Mark Rylance

THE BIG SECRET LIVE
'I AM SHAKESPEARE'
WEBCAM DAYTIME CHATROOM SHOW!

A Comedy of Shakespearean Identity Crisis

NICK HERN BOOKS
London
www.nickhernbooks.co.uk

A Nick Hern Book

I Am Shakespeare first published in Great Britain as a paperback original in 2012 by Nick Hern Books Limited, The Glasshouse, 49a Goldhawk Road, London W12 8QP

Reprinted 2013

Production photograph © Alastair Muir
Cover image: SWD (www.swd.uk.com)
Cover design: Ned Hoste, 2H

Typeset by Nick Hern Books, London
Printed in the UK by Mimeo Ltd, Huntingdon, Cambridgeshire PE29 6XX

A CIP catalogue record for this book is available from the British Library

ISBN   978 1 84842 269 8

MARK RYLANCE

Mark Rylance is an actor, theatre director, and writer. He spent his youth in America and returned to England in 1978 to train at RADA under Hugh Cruttwell. In 1980 the Glasgow Citizens Theatre gave him his first job, a year in repertoire, a trip to the carnival in Venice with Goldoni, and an Equity card.

He played Hamlet at ages sixteen, in Milwaukee, Wisconsin, twenty-eight to thirty, at the Royal Shakespeare Company, and forty at Shakespeare's Globe. In the early eighties he and a group of actors formed a theatre company, the London Theatre of Imagination which evolved into Phoebus Cart. In 1991 he played Prospero in Phoebus Cart's production of *The Tempest* at the Rollright Stones, and on the Globe building site. That year Sam Wanamaker invited him to join the Artistic Directorate and he subsequently became the Artistic Director of Shakespeare's Globe from 1995 to 2005. During his career he has played in fifty productions of plays by Shakespeare and his contemporaries. He has also appeared on Broadway, in many English theatres, and on film and television.

Mark is an honorary bencher of the Middle Temple Hall, chairman of the Shakespearean Authorship Trust, a friend of the Francis Bacon Trust, President of the Marlowe Society, a Patron and Ambassador of Survival, the movement for tribal people, and Peace Direct, working for non-violent resolution of conflict.

Colin Hurley as William Shakspar and Mark Rylance as Frank
in the original production of I Am Shakespeare,
at the Minerva Theatre, Chichester, 2007

Introduction

The Big Secret Live 'I Am Shakespeare' Webcam Daytime Chatroom Show was created in the summer of 2007 for the Chichester Festival Theatre. Greg Ripley-Duggan produced the play, and subsequent to our run in Chichester, organised a brief tour to Warwickshire, Oxford and Cambridge University, amongst other places. This was not unlike taking a play that questioned Robert Burns's identity as a poet, to Scotland. But, for some reason, the Shakespeare authorship controversy pierces deep to the heart of identity for some people, wherever you play. It was the extreme reaction of otherwise reasonable people that inspired this play. Their efforts to repress my curiosity, and frighten others away from the mystery, were funny in retrospect but extremely trying at the time, especially when I was Artistic Director of Shakespeare's Globe Theatre in London between 1995 and 2005.

I say that the play was 'created', as I had only written the first act and some of the second when the cast gathered in the Soho Laundry to begin rehearsals that summer. Under Matthew Warchus's excellent direction, which included many improvements and developments of the script and idea, we then created the play. All of the original cast, especially Sean Foley who played Barry, improvised lines and situations, which I later included in the text. I am indebted to this spirit of adventure and collaboration, which, by the way, has always been my image of an aspect of the creation of the Shakespeare plays as well.

The play is set in the then present: 2007. I am writing this introduction to the published text in 2012. Some things have happened since in the world of Shakespearean authorship studies that probably warrant mention in a new production – James Shapiro's book, *Contested Will*, and others. Frank, in the play, would certainly be aware of the Roland Emmerich film, *Anonymous*, and the fuss it generated, not least the website created by the Shakespeare Birthplace Trust, 'Shakespeare Bites Back', which has some passing similarities to Frank's own website. I wonder if anyone came to our play from the Birthplace Trust when we played down the road in Warwick University. Professor Jonathan Bate, of that university, soon after created his own play with Simon Callow called *Being Shakespeare*. When I mount a new production I will probably update the script, and will be able to offer the new material I create. It is also always a possibility to produce the play as a period piece set in 2007. As much as things have changed in the sphere of authorship studies, the technology of computers has changed even more. This also needs to be born in mind. Allowing the audience to send text messages, instead of, or as well as, phoning in to the show, might be a good idea.

I am also indebted to the many independent and professional Shakespeare scholars whose work has fascinated me since I first began to develop my reasonable doubt that the actor William Shakspar wrote the plays: Peter Dawkins, Diana Price, Robin Williams, Professor William Leahy, Charles Beauclerk, Stephanie Hopkins Hughes, Mike Frohnsdorff, Professor Daniel Wright, Professor William Rubinstein, Professor Stanley Wells, Professor Jonathan Bate, Nigel Cockburn, Michael Wood, John Shahan, to name a few of the many people whose work has inspired me. This is to neglect the many before my time who have loved Shakespeare's work in such a way that they felt they must inquire about its origin, including a few in his own time brave enough to hint at the mystery: Ben Jonson in particular. I am also indebted to David Canter, the author of a book on the mystery of Jack the Ripper, *Mapping Murder*. A good read for the actor playing the sergeant.

As the play involves improvised interaction with the audience, it is recommended that the actors playing Shakspar, Sidney, Bacon and Oxford read as much as they can about their character's authorship case. I have endeavoured to write each character as if they wrote the plays themselves, singularly or collaboratively. The Shakespearean Authorship Trust (SAT) has an excellent website on which books are recommended on each candidate. I would recommend Beauclerk and Hopkins Hughes on Oxford, Dawkins and Cockburn on Bacon, Williams on Mary Sidney, and on Shakspar? Take your pick. Diana Price is the best on why there is a question at all. Mark Twain, the funniest. The

Declaration of Reasonable Doubt at www.doubtaboutwill.org is a clear statement also of why there is a question.

My apologies to those who champion other candidates, especially Christopher Marlowe, Neville, and Derby. There was not time to do their cases justice. But, ultimately, the play is more concerned with the search for identity, our own identity, than the search for the identity of the author of the Shakespeare works.

The whole adventure was initially inspired by the brilliant American TV show, *Meeting of Minds*, created by the genius host, Steve Allen. I used to work on the play in my dressing room at the Comedy Theatre in London's West End, while performing in the farce *Boeing-Boeing*. The director, John Dove, was a great encouragement during this period. Curiously, if my memory serves me right, *I Am Shakespeare* had as much laughter, if not more at times, as *Boeing-Boeing*. Those times did not include the performances at Warwick University, where the students were actively discouraged from attending, and the audience was, shall we say, deconstructed.

Needless to say, I love Shakespeare – the work and the author – more than any other human art I have ever encountered. I have made my living, in many more ways than an actor's pay check, on Shakespeare, since I was sixteen years old (which was thirty years ago at the time I wrote this play). I do not believe, as was charged against me at the Globe, that I am biting the hand that fed me. I am attempting to shake it. The fact that Shakespeare's work will all disappear from the universe one day is more awe-inspiring to me than my own death.

But what a laugh we had making this. I will never forget it. Rehearsing from ten till six. Home for dinner and then writing until my head literally fell to the desk at three or four in the morning. Thanks to all who believed it was worthwhile to ask, 'Who's there?'

And to all those audience members who stood at the end of the play and shouted 'I am Shakespeare' – You are.

Mark Rylance

Production Note

The action of the play takes place entirely in and around Frank Charlton's garage, on the outskirts of Maidstone, Kent, on the day that the play happens to be performed.

The play begins in the early evening and concludes later that night. It is a rainy night with lightning and thunder.

The telephone on Frank's desk is live and the number is real. At the top of the show an announcement invites the audience to please leave their mobile telephones switched on throughout the play and to ring the actors whenever they wish. The telephone number remains visible on the large television screens hanging above the garage set. (Though sometimes, I have to confess, we had to close the telephone line to let the action flow, and because certain members of the audience wrote the number down and telephoned from home the next night, which seemed like a scripted phone call to the present audience. It would be good to resolve this slight issue.)

These screens also project images from the camera filming live inside the garage, the webcam inside Frank's refrigerator in his house, and other documentary and pictorial evidence from Frank's laptop.

I recommend a thrust stage as it helps if the audience can see one another.

The Elizabethan characters should all appear in authentic reconstructions of the clothes they might have worn when alive at the age they appear. The Shakespearean Authorship Trust (SAT) owns the clothes of the authors worn in the original production. Their construction would not have been possible without the generous donation of Antoinette Abbey and the exquisite skill of our designer Jenny Tiramani and her tailors.

You will need to get permission to use a few minutes of the film *Spartacus* by Dalton Trumbo. It cost us just over six hundred pounds sterling, but is well worth it. Actually, it is essential.

Claire van Kampen wrote excellent music for the play, which I would recommend, especially Barry Wild's *Top of the Pops* hit 'I'm a Sputnik Love God'.

I feel it is probably too long. When was a play ever too short? Especially one connected to Shakespeare. I have indicated some cuts in the text (marked within square brackets) and would suggest producers explore more cuts. There is undoubtedly too much information, but I have left it in for you to decide what would be best for the given audience you will encounter, not unlike a Shakespeare play, though in that aspect only.

Author's Note

With thanks to my wife, the beautiful Claire van Kampen, and to Juliet and Nataasha, the two lovely daughters whom I co-father with the gentle Chris van Kampen. The play is dedicated to them with my deep affection.

Mark Rylance

Characters

FRANK CHARLTON, *a schoolteacher and Shakespearean authorship researcher, who was once a star Shakespeare academic at Oxford or Cambridge University. Age around fifty. Obsessed.*

BARRY WILD, *Frank's next-door neighbour. A pop star, who once had a top-twenty hit entitled 'I'm a Sputnik Love God'. Very interested in crop circles and popular culture. Age around thirty-five to forty-five. Affable.*

WILLIAM SHAKSPAR, *born 1564. Died 1616. Posthumously attributed with writing the plays and poems of William Shakespeare. Age forty to forty-five. Confident, unassuming Warwickshire actor.*

FRANCIS BACON, *born 1560. Died 1626. Elizabethan statesman, philosopher, lawyer, father of modern science, concealed poet. Believed by some to have written the plays and poems of Shakespeare. Age sixty. Wise, witty, mystic.*

EDWARD DE VERE, *the seventeenth Earl of Oxford. Also believed by some, including Freud, to have written the plays of William Shakespeare. Passionate, depressed, very much like Hamlet actually. Dressed in extraordinary Italian fashion. Age twenty-six to thirty-five. Dangerous.*

SERGEANT TREVOR FREEMAN, *Kent County Constabulary. Very interested in Jack the Ripper. Not thought to have anything to do with the plays and poems of William Shakespeare.*

LADY MARY SIDNEY, *the Countess of Pembroke, sister to the famous poet Sir Philip Sydney. A poet and dramatist in her own right, she founded the Wilton School of English Writing on the banks of the River Avon, Wiltshire. Often called 'The Swan', and believed by some to have been part of a group of writers who wrote the plays and poems of Shakespeare. Age twenty-five to thirty. Witty, beautiful, with a profound grief beneath.*

THE SERGEANT'S TWIN BROTHER, *an angry, orthodox boar of a Shakespearean.*

TELEPHONE SALESMAN

I Am Shakespeare was first performed at the Minerva Theatre, Chichester, on 14 August 2007. The cast was as follows:

FRANK CHARLTON	Mark Rylance
BARRY WILD	Sean Foley
WILLIAM SHAKSPAR	Colin Hurley
FRANCIS BACON	Roddy Maude Roxby
EDWARD DE VERE	Alex Hassell
SERGEANT TREVOR	Sam Parks
FREEMAN / HIS TWIN /	
TELEPHONE SALESMAN	
LADY MARY SIDNEY	Juliet Rylance

Director	Matthew Warchus
Designer	Jenny Tiramani
Composer	Claire van Kampen
Sound Designer	Simon Baker
Lighting Designer	Paul Pyant
Choreographer	Sian Williams
Dialect Coach	Penny Dyer

ACT ONE

Scene One

Frank Arrives for His Weekly Broadcast

A driveway and garage in Maidstone, Kent.

Early evening. The present.

It's raining hard as FRANK CHARLTON *arrives on his bicycle, sheltering a large pile of school papers for correction under his plastic poncho. He is all flashing lights and reflector strips. Inside the garage, the phone on his desk is ringing, and then the answerphone message can be heard.*

FRANK. Oh God.

As FRANK *enters the garage we hear his neighbour,* BARRY, *leaving a message.*

BARRY (*on answerphone*). Hello, Frank. Are you there?

FRANK chooses not to pick up the phone.

FRANK. Barry, I told you not to use the chat-show hotline.

BARRY. I know you told me not to ring on your chat-show hotline. Are you there? I've left some tunes on my Korg for the opening theme. They're in the keyboard memory under 'Chat-room-Garage-Music 1590's style'; one, two, and three. This rain's pouring all over my conservatory. There's leaks everywhere. So I've got to get up to the drains and clear them out. Live up. Bazza. Hope the jokes work.

FRANK gathers his school papers into a pile and hurries to prepare himself and the garage, multitasking at great speed. Possible tasks include:

Audibly searching through the Korg keyboard for the opening theme music.

Hearing and rejecting BARRY*'s suggested music for the opening of his chat show.*

Changing from his rain poncho and worn grey teaching suit into his host clothes; the blue Who's There? *T-shirt.*

Selecting and arranging the books and notes for the show.

Practising parts of his opening gambit out loud, 'Stratfordians!', etc.

Clearing boxes from the guest seating, weekend gardening debris, and tools, off the visible set.

Setting up the Minerva Britannia curtain frame on the desk and other props. And then focusing the web cameras and lights.

Lowering the painted backdrop tied to a ceiling crossbar, behind his desk.

Finally putting on his Steve Allen-style, chat-show glasses, and sitting.

While FRANK *desperately sets all this up, the chat-show phone rings again on his chat-show desk and he eventually, in great frustration, answers it. A fast T-Mobile salesman from Madras is on the line. We hear the conversation, as we have heard* BARRY's *message over the chat-show's phone speaker.*

FRANK. Barry. That music is wrong. I said classic tunes…

SALESMAN. Is that Mrs Carlton?

FRANK. Oh. No, this is Frank Charlton and you're through to *Who's There?* The International Shakespeare Authorship show. We're not live on air, but what's your question?

SALESMAN. Hello. Are you Mr Carlton?

FRANK. Charlton. Yes, Frank Charlton.

SALESMAN. All right, Frank. Are you having good weather there, Frank?

FRANK. No, it's dreadful, raining. Why, what's the weather like where you are?

SALESMAN. Here, it's very hot and lovely, thank you very much, Frank.

FRANK. Hot and lovely. Where are you?

SALESMAN. Madras.

FRANK. Madras. What is this, some kind of sales pitch?

SALESMAN. No, Frank, this is a free package offer.

FRANK. How did you get this number?

SALESMAN. All right, Frank, you are on our list, Frank.

FRANK. Please don't call me Frank. You don't even know me.

SALESMAN. Yes, I do, Frank.

FRANK. What colour hair have I got?

SALESMAN. Dark hair.

FRANK. You're just guessing. This is the problem with the whole world. No one knows anyone else. We meet at the end of wires, and guess about each other.

SALESMAN. Frank. If you purchased a mobile phone, you would meet people without wires.

FRANK. I don't want to buy a mobile phone. Don't call me Frank. You know nothing about me. You just think you know me because of something someone else has written about me on some list, which you have taken for granted to be true. You're probably a Stratfordian.

SALESMAN. What's a Stratfordian?

FRANK. A Stratfordian? A Stratfordian is someone who believes that the actor from Stratford-upon-Avon wrote *Love's Labour's Lost*, for example.

SALESMAN. Didn't he?

FRANK. Exactly. Why do you think that? Because someone told you to think that. Did you ever question it? No. You just bought it hook, line and sinker. Have you ever wondered how the man from Stratford could possibly have written *Love's Labour's Lost*?

SALESMAN. No. How could he have done it?

FRANK. With extreme difficulty, I would imagine, when he has only just arrived in London, from God knows where, so how could he have ever developed the vocabulary and wit and learning of a university-educated playwright? How could he have learnt such intimate details of the Royal Court of Navarre in France?

SALESMAN. I don't know. I never thought about it, Frank. It sounds impossible.

FRANK. Well, there you are. You never thought about it.

SALESMAN. Yes, I see. That's amazing. Frank, you've convinced me.

FRANK. Really?

SALESMAN. Yes. Frank. *Love's Labour's Lost* is very like *Friends*, isn't it?

FRANK. *Friends*?

SALESMAN. Yes. You know you can watch *Friends* on your T-Mobile network phone for only sixteen pounds ninety-nine pence a month.

FRANK *hangs up. We hear the chimes of six o'clock.*

Scene Two

The Big Secret Chat-Show Opening Gambit

As FRANK *hangs up the telephone, the clock strikes the hour.*

We see FRANK *hurriedly prepare to start the show. He turns the camera on and a dark picture appears on the internet screens hanging above the set in the theatre.*

From behind the proscenium, his arm reaches out quickly through the curtain with a remote control that he aims at the CD player and the lights. Pre-arranged theme music begins to

play, and lights come up on the proscenium and curtain that
FRANK *has placed on his desk. The image appears on the*
screens above.

FRANK'*s hand and arm, in an Elizabethan sleeve with lace,*
extends through the curtain holding a feather, as if to complete
the writing on the scroll of parchment before him.

He begins to speak ominously in two voices from behind the
curtain, while he points with the feather to the Latin heraldry
around the frame. The two voices are his imagination of an
actor speaking the first line in Hamlet *and his own host voice.*

FRANK. Who's there?

Pointing to 'MENTE VIDEBORI'.

Mente Videbori! By the mind I shall be seen!

NAY ANSWER ME?

Pointing to 'VIVITUR IN GENIO'.

Vivitur in Genio! One lives in one's genius.

STAND AND UNFOLD YOURSELF!

Pointing to 'CAETERA MORTIS ERUNT', with the help of
his other modern arm as he can't reach round with the
Elizabethan arm.

Caetera Mortis Erunt! All else passes away.

Opening the curtain and sticking his head through.

Ladies and gentlemen, wherever you are on the World Wide
Web, you come most carefully upon your hour, for 'tis now
struck six, and 'tis time to welcome each and every one of
you to another international broadcast of *Who's There?* The
only live internet chat-room show that dares to ask the
question 'Who really wrote the plays of William
Shakespeare?' The first in our brand-new season.

FRANK *presses an applause pedal with his foot, and*
blackout with his remote. Music swells. In the darkness,
FRANK *lifts the prop curtain frame out off the desk. He sits*
down, straightens himself and brings up the show lighting
state while also fading the music with another remote.

Running across the top of the screen or appearing at intervals are the words:

'*Don't be like the rest – silent. You can call or text Frank right now on 0845-475-1564.*'

'*I want to hear your views! Calls are charged at local rates.*'

FRANK *reads from cards like David Letterman.*

Hello. I'm Frank Charlton, your host tonight.

FRANK *starts mystery music and points to a list of names and faces stuck on a board:*

'*Henry James, Ralph Waldo Emerson, John Galsworthy, Lord Palmerston, Benjamin Disraeli, Sir Tyrone Guthrie, Mark Twain, Walt Whitman, Charles Dickens, Sir John Gielgud, Charlie Chaplin, Orson Welles, Dr Sigmund Freud, Daphne du Maurier, and Sir Derek Jacobi.*'

Mark Twain, Walt Whitman, Charles Dickens, Sir John Gielgud, Charlie Chaplin…

BARRY, FRANK'*s neighbour, enters the garage through the back door, trying not to disturb.*

Barry? Orson Welles, Dr Sigmund Freud, Daphne du Maurier, Sir Derek Jacobi, and all the rest.

Who are they? What do all these famous people have in common?

BARRY. Guttering.

FRANK. What?

BARRY. Have you got any guttering?

FRANK. I don't know. I'm live on *air*, Barry.

BARRY *gets out the stepladder.*

They are all people who have expressed doubt that the actor William Shakespeare wrote the plays. That's right. We're just reasonable people, with a reasonable doubt. Are you one of us?

There is a teddy bear attached to the camera tripod.

BARRY. Talk to teddy! Don't just talk at the camera, like that. Talk as if you're really talking with someone. Talk to teddy! Lighten up. Relax. Tell them about the jokes and the special guest.

FRANK plays a piece of music to show he's not all doom and gloom.

FRANK. Now, to show you that we authorship researchers aren't all doom and gloom, something new this season: the Best Authorship Joke Competition!

Applause.

All right. My producers have just agreed that the winner of this competition will get to be a guest on the show! Fancy being on the show with someone like my super-special guest this evening?

He uncovers a cardboard cut-out of the upper body of Kenneth Branagh, which was pre-placed on the guest chair next to the desk. He adjusts the camera to pick up the guest.

Kenneth Branagh!

BARRY. And use the sound effects I gave you.

BARRY taps the sound-effect pedal. We hear a loud hysterical voice saying, 'That's funny, that's really funny!'

No, the other one!

He taps the 'Dive, dive!' submarine sound effect, and then the ecstatic applause button, and FRANK stops the music. Very upset.

FRANK. No, Barry! This is what I'm talking about. Unrehearsed technical bits. It doesn't give the right impression.

BARRY. Sorry, Frank.

Silence.

FRANK. It's not an entertainment.

Silence.

BARRY. I'd just like to say to anyone out there that, since you started doing *Who's There?*, the Shakespeare authorship question has really changed the way I look at everything.

FRANK. Really?

BARRY. Yes, I can't think of any part of my life that hasn't been affected.

FRANK. You've never said that before. Thanks. Can you give us an example of how it's affected your life?

Pause.

BARRY. Can I think about that and get back to you?

FRANK. Certainly. May I just say, Barry, that you are the best musical director I could get. Really. The best in Maidstone. I don't think there are many internet chat shows that have a musical director who's had a top-twenty hit.

BARRY. Oh, don't embarrass me, Frank. (*Sotto*.) Mention *Top of the Pops*.

FRANK. Oh yes. Barry here was on *Top of the Pops*. When was that, Barry?

BARRY. Oh, I can't remember. May the 17th, 1985.

FRANK. With his unforgettable hit song… 'God loves spunky… spotty knick-knacks'?

BARRY. 'I Am a Sputnik Love God'.

FRANK. Terrific. And twenty-two years later, here you are, still churning out the hits.

BARRY. Well, I…

BARRY *gives him a look. To break the moment,* FRANK *steps on the submarine sound effect.* BARRY *exits.*

FRANK. Oh no! You know what that means, ladies and gentlemen! It's time for the first of our TOP-TEN LIST OF REASONS TO QUESTION THE AUTHORSHIP OF THE SHAKESPEARE PLAYS. Thanks for dropping by, Barry. Ladies and gentlemen, Barry Wild.

FRANK sets off applause and then new music. 'Whole Lotta Love' by Led Zeppelin. He lifts a bust of William Shakespeare onto the desk, opens the head and reaches inside.

I'll just reach into my Shakespeare or Bust and see what comes out first!

So, Reason Number Ten.

If the actor from Stratford-upon-Avon wrote the sonnets, plays and poems of Shakespeare, which contain the largest vocabulary of any known writer in history, over twenty-five thousand words – that's more than three times the vocabulary used in the King James Bible – including nearly two thousand new words never written before – if those plays are drawn from well over a hundred books in Latin, French, Spanish, Italian, and Greek – if those plays are so accurate about life that specialists in at least thirty-one specialist subjects, from soldiering to navigation at sea… In fact, here they are on the bottom of your screen.

Across the bottom of the internet screens we can read a running list of all the subjects that are accurately described or employed by the author of the Shakespeare plays.

You see… they're going a bit fast to read but… there they are… ranging from esoteric Neoplatonic philosophy to… angling; all those specialists assert that the author must have had direct experience of their subject…

The question is HOW, HOW, HOW did that small-town actor acquire all this knowledge and life experience?

WHAT DOES FRANK SAY?

You can be born with genius, folks, but you can't be born with book-learning or life experience.

Picking up a First Folio with a picture of Shakespeare on the front.

Mr Shakespeare, at present your life story and the book-learning and life experience in these plays, don't match.

FRANK. Have you been sent here by the Shakespeare Birthplace Trust?

SHAKSPAR. No.

FRANK. The Shakespeare Institute?

SHAKSPAR. No.

FRANK *begins to speak.*

No.

FRANK. Is this some sort of joke?

SHAKSPAR. You can't fathom me, can you? Do you really think people have to be extraordinary themselves to do extraordinary things? I lived a thousand *extraordinary* lives in my writing – so many kings, lovers, murderers. They tired me out, Frank. But that's not who I am.

FRANK. You dress up as William Shakespeare, break into my studio, hijack my show and then…

SHAKSPAR. It's time you stopped, Frank. Please. Let it go. I don't want to be man of the millennium. I just want a good millennium sleep. Every time you challenge me, some fool starts another penetrating biography: 'Closer to Shakespeare', 'Shakespeare, The Player', 'Shakespeare, The Lost Years', 'Shakespeare for All Time'. Each one's like an electric shock in my sleep, waking me up again. If I had known what it's like to be a ghost, I never would have given them such small parts.

We see BARRY *running round the outside of the garage.*

FRANK. You think you can come in here, pretending to be William Shakespeare, sabotage my show…

BARRY *rushes in.*

The phone on FRANK's *desk starts ringing.* FRANK *looks at it in surprise.*

Fantastic! The phones are ringing. Stay with us, ladies and gentlemen. Let's take some calls and move this historic debate forward.

Picking up the phone.

Hello. This is Frank Charlton, your host on *Who's There?* What's your question?

We hear BARRY *speaking with a thick Scottish accent.*

BARRY. Hello, this is Derek Jacobi.

FRANK. Derek Jacobi?

BARRY. Yes, Derek Jacobi.

FRANK. Oh my God… Derek? I mean, Sir Jacobi. I left a message last year, but I never thought you would call back…

Pause.

Do you mean Sir Derek Jacobi the actor or another man with the same name?

BARRY. Yes, the actor. It's me, actor Sir Derek Jacobi.

FRANK. I didn't know you were Scottish?

BARRY. Yes, Scottish.

Pause.

Hold on, I'm just putting on my porridge… oh, I love some salt in my porridge… there we go. Now, I just wanted to say how much I enjoy your show…

FRANK. Barry?

Silence.

For God's sake, Barry. You've no idea the day I've had today. I've got a meeting in the morning with the headmaster and loads of parents; accused of upsetting the boys' fragile sense of identity by questioning the identity of Shakespeare in class.

BARRY. How did you know it was me?

FRANK. Derek Jacobi's not Scottish.

BARRY. It's the only accent I can do. I thought it might help.

FRANK. Well, it didn't.

He hangs up. Looks at the camera.

FRANK *takes down a framed letter from the back wall of the set and approaches the camera downstage on its tripod. His face and the letter appear as large as possible on the screens above.*

You see this, ladies and gentlemen? Do you know what it is? This is the letter rejecting my PhD by one of our top universities.

And do you want to know why my PhD was rejected? Here's the title: *The Identity of the Author of the Shakespeare Works? A Question of Reasonable Doubt.* That's right. The one question you can't ask at university. The one question you are not allowed to ask on the International Shakespeare Website. Wikipedia!

I mean, it's like telling Galileo that he can look at the heavens through his telescope but only if he looks at the moon! As long as an open inquiry into the cause of these works is suppressed, how can we really understand their incredible beauty and humanity? As long as this unbelievable situation exists, this rejection letter stays framed on my wall and I stay here... still searching for the true identity of William Shakespeare!

Scene Three

The First Guest Ever: William Shakespeare

There are two knocks on the door.

FRANK. Who's there?

SHAKSPAR. Frank.

FRANK. Who is it?

WILLIAM SHAKSPAR *enters.*

SHAKSPAR. Hello, Frank.

FRANK. Who are you?

SHAKSPAR. Who do you think I am?

FRANK. Who do you think you are?

SHAKSPAR. No, who do *you* think I am? And more to t' point, *why* do you think I am anyone other than who actually am?

FRANK. What?

SHAKSPAR. Why do you do it, Frank?

FRANK. Why do I do what?

SHAKSPAR. Why do you get yourself in such a twis' who I am? Haven't you got better things to do? Y need this to make you special. You should be pro just an ordinary good old teacher like your father

FRANK. How do you know I'm a teacher? How do my father's name?

SHAKSPAR. So what's this all about? Books, boo you know there are more books about my play there are about the Bible? But then, I had a hea wasn't an English Bible until a few years after

Scene Four

The Interruption of the Neighbour's Musical Genius

SHAKSPAR *looks at the books.*

BARRY *enters, making sure he doesn't forget a song he's just composed in his head.*

BARRY. I've got a song, Frank. After I rang you I went out with the guttering and BAM! I'VE GOT IT! After twenty-two years, my follow-up! 'Long Green Summer Grass'. It's got it all. Love in the afternoon. The great flood. It's like a green love anthem. Sort of Al Gore meets Barry White!

SHAKSPAR. Hello, Barry.

BARRY *sees* SHAKSPAR.

BARRY. What are you doing?

FRANK. What are you doing?

[BARRY. Who's that?

FRANK. Yes. Who's that?

BARRY. Why?

FRANK. Why what?

BARRY. What?

FRANK. Why?]

BARRY. Why do something like this without telling me? Hiring a lookalike. I don't think that's very professional, you know, to keep secrets from your musical director. I thought we were working together on this. Oh, fuck it! Fuck it! I've forgotten the fucking song! I've forgotten the fucking tune! Look what you've done. I can't remember it. It's gone.

SHAKSPAR (*singing*).
>Come on, baby, come on, baby, don't say maybe,
>When you're way down, let me lay down –

BARRY. That's my song!

SHAKSPAR (*singing*).
>Lay down with you in the summer grass,
>In the long green summer grass.

BARRY. That's the song I just made up!

SHAKSPAR (*singing*).
>I'm changing my drains down,
>So, baby, when it rains down,
>Ain't no summer hose ban's gonna turn,
>Gonna burn, my long green summer grass to brown.

I thought the repeats helped the rhythm.

BARRY. Who is this guy, Frank?

FRANK. Why don't you both just stop pretending. Get out. Go on, get out, the both of you.

BARRY. I never met the man before in my life! I swear on Brian May's plectrum!

Scene Five

The First Interview Ever with William Shakespeare

SHAKSPAR. May I just finish this before I go?

BARRY. Do you know any more of my songs?

SHAKSPAR. Yes, but what I like best is that children's book you're working on.

FRANK. You never told me you were working on a children's book.

BARRY. I never told anyone about *Teddy and the Philosopher's Guitar*. What are you, like, a professional mind-reader? Is that your act?

SHAKSPAR. In a way, I suppose I always was, but since I died...

FRANK. Listen, you Shakespeare Kissogram, lookalike fake, bald-headed bladder-faced Midlands Pranny...

BARRY. Hey, Frank, why don't you give him a chance to explain himself.

SHAKSPAR. Because his mind is closed, Barry. He doesn't want to know who wrote the plays. He wants to know he's right. And I think he's probably got some kind of hang-up about common people creating great works of art.

SHAKSPAR *gets up to go*.

BARRY. Now you're talking.

FRANK. No I haven't.

SHAKSPAR. I'm off now. (*Speaking into the camera*.) May I just say thank you to everyone, actors and audiences everywhere, for making my plays the big success they are. I never imagined they would last so long.

FRANK (*also into the camera*). Because he never imagined them in the first place.

SHAKSPAR. I think I might go up to Stratford-upon-Avon and visit the Birthplace Trust. What's the best way to get there?

BARRY. How did you get here?

SHAKSPAR. I don't know... something to do with the internet and the weather? Look, I've written something for you, Frank. Just to show you there's no hard feelings. One of your favourite sonnets. You wouldn't believe the money you can get for any old document connected to me nowadays.

SHAKSPAR *puts it on the desk*.

FRANK. Oh, very impressive. Phoney Elizabethan writing. You've been up all night rehearsing this.

SHAKSPAR. Don't you want a handwritten sonnet?

FRANK. No, I don't want your lousy homework.

> FRANK *tears it up and throws it in his face. Sniffs him.*

> By the way, I don't know if your friends have told you, but you have got severe hygiene issues.

SHAKSPAR. I'll make my own way. Fare thee well, Barry.

BARRY. Fare thee well, Will.

SHAKSPAR. I'm retired; I just want to be left alone, like Prospero. Let your indulgence set me free.

FRANK. If Shakespeare's so like Prospero, why didn't he educate his daughters?

SHAKSPAR. They didn't want to be educated.

FRANK. Why didn't he write or receive any letters?

SHAKSPAR. I conducted my business in person.

FRANK. Why did Shakespeare never write about his home town, Stratford?

SHAKSPAR. Which would you rather go and hear: *The Tragedy of Hamlet, Prince of Denmark*, or *The Slightly Embarrassing Day in the Life of John, Glove Maker of Stratford*?

> *He goes out and they carry on talking around and out in front of the garage.*

FRANK. People in Stratford had no idea he was a playwright?

SHAKSPAR. I kept myself to myself.

FRANK. Then, why was he so litigious?

SHAKSPAR. What's any of this got to do with my work?

FRANK. That's exactly my question.

BARRY. Will, you know you can see inside my head, can you see inside Frank's?

SHAKSPAR. When? In the past, present or future? Once you die, your existence is not bound by time or space.

The phone on FRANK'*s desk starts ringing.* FRANK *looks at it in surprise.*

Fantastic! The phones are ringing. Stay with us, ladies and gentlemen. Let's take some calls and move this historic debate forward.

Picking up the phone.

Hello. This is Frank Charlton, your host on *Who's There?* What's your question?

We hear BARRY *speaking with a thick Scottish accent.*

BARRY. Hello, this is Derek Jacobi.

FRANK. Derek Jacobi?

BARRY. Yes, Derek Jacobi.

FRANK. Oh my God... Derek? I mean, Sir Jacobi. I left a message last year, but I never thought you would call back...

Pause.

Do you mean Sir Derek Jacobi the actor or another man with the same name?

BARRY. Yes, the actor. It's me, actor Sir Derek Jacobi.

FRANK. I didn't know you were Scottish?

BARRY. Yes, Scottish.

Pause.

Hold on, I'm just putting on my porridge... oh, I love some salt in my porridge... there we go. Now, I just wanted to say how much I enjoy your show...

FRANK. Barry?

Silence.

For God's sake, Barry. You've no idea the day I've had today. I've got a meeting in the morning with the headmaster and loads of parents; accused of upsetting the boys' fragile sense of identity by questioning the identity of Shakespeare in class.

BARRY. How did you know it was me?

FRANK. Derek Jacobi's not Scottish.

BARRY. It's the only accent I can do. I thought it might help.

FRANK. Well, it didn't.

He hangs up. Looks at the camera.

FRANK *takes down a framed letter from the back wall of the set and approaches the camera downstage on its tripod. His face and the letter appear as large as possible on the screens above.*

You see this, ladies and gentlemen? Do you know what it is? This is the letter rejecting my PhD by one of our top universities.

And do you want to know why my PhD was rejected? Here's the title: *The Identity of the Author of the Shakespeare Works? A Question of Reasonable Doubt.* That's right. The one question you can't ask at university. The one question you are not allowed to ask on the International Shakespeare Website. Wikipedia!

I mean, it's like telling Galileo that he can look at the heavens through his telescope but only if he looks at the moon! As long as an open inquiry into the cause of these works is suppressed, how can we really understand their incredible beauty and humanity? As long as this unbelievable situation exists, this rejection letter stays framed on my wall and I stay here... still searching for the true identity of William Shakespeare!

Scene Three

The First Guest Ever: William Shakespeare

There are two knocks on the door.

FRANK. Who's there?

SHAKSPAR. Frank.

FRANK. Who is it?

   WILLIAM SHAKSPAR *enters*.

SHAKSPAR. Hello, Frank.

FRANK. Who are you?

SHAKSPAR. Who do you think I am?

FRANK. Who do you think you are?

SHAKSPAR. No, who do *you* think I am? And more to the point, *why* do you think I am anyone other than who I actually am?

FRANK. What?

SHAKSPAR. Why do you do it, Frank?

FRANK. Why do I do what?

SHAKSPAR. Why do you get yourself in such a twist about who I am? Haven't you got better things to do? You don't need this to make you special. You should be proud of being just an ordinary good old teacher like your father, Tom.

FRANK. How do you know I'm a teacher? How do you know my father's name?

SHAKSPAR. So what's this all about? Books, books, books. Do you know there are more books about my play *Hamlet* than there are about the Bible? But then, I had a head start. There wasn't an English Bible until a few years after *Hamlet*.

FRANK. Have you been sent here by the Shakespeare
    Birthplace Trust?

SHAKSPAR. No.

FRANK. The Shakespeare Institute?

SHAKSPAR. No.

   FRANK *begins to speak*.

   No.

FRANK. Is this some sort of joke?

SHAKSPAR. You can't fathom me, can you? Do you really
    think people have to be extraordinary themselves to do
    extraordinary things? I lived a thousand *extraordinary* lives
    in my writing – so many kings, lovers, murderers. They tired
    me out, Frank. But that's not who I am.

FRANK. You dress up as William Shakespeare, break into my
    studio, hijack my show and then...

SHAKSPAR. It's time you stopped, Frank. Please. Let it go. I
    don't want to be man of the millennium. I just want a good
    millennium sleep. Every time you challenge me, some fool
    starts another penetrating biography: 'Closer to
    Shakespeare', 'Shakespeare, The Player', 'Shakespeare, The
    Lost Years', 'Shakespeare for All Time'. Each one's like an
    electric shock in my sleep, waking me up again. If I had
    known what it's like to be a ghost, I never would have given
    them such small parts.

   We see BARRY *running round the outside of the garage*.

FRANK. You think you can come in here, pretending to be
    William Shakespeare, sabotage my show...

   BARRY *rushes in*.

Scene Four

The Interruption of the Neighbour's Musical Genius

SHAKSPAR *looks at the books.*

BARRY *enters, making sure he doesn't forget a song he's just composed in his head.*

BARRY. I've got a song, Frank. After I rang you I went out with the guttering and BAM! I'VE GOT IT! After twenty-two years, my follow-up! 'Long Green Summer Grass'. It's got it all. Love in the afternoon. The great flood. It's like a green love anthem. Sort of Al Gore meets Barry White!

SHAKSPAR. Hello, Barry.

BARRY *sees* SHAKSPAR.

BARRY. What are you doing?

FRANK. What are you doing?

[BARRY. Who's that?

FRANK. Yes. Who's that?

BARRY. Why?

FRANK. Why what?

BARRY. What?

FRANK. Why?]

BARRY. Why do something like this without telling me? Hiring a lookalike. I don't think that's very professional, you know, to keep secrets from your musical director. I thought we were working together on this. Oh, fuck it! Fuck it! I've forgotten the fucking song! I've forgotten the fucking tune! Look what you've done. I can't remember it. It's gone.

SHAKSPAR (*singing*).
> Come on, baby, come on, baby, don't say maybe,
> When you're way down, let me lay down –

BARRY. That's my song!

SHAKSPAR (*singing*).
> Lay down with you in the summer grass,
> In the long green summer grass.

BARRY. That's the song I just made up!

SHAKSPAR (*singing*).
> I'm changing my drains down,
> So, baby, when it rains down,
> Ain't no summer hose ban's gonna turn,
> Gonna burn, my long green summer grass to brown.

I thought the repeats helped the rhythm.

BARRY. Who is this guy, Frank?

FRANK. Why don't you both just stop pretending. Get out. Go on, get out, the both of you.

BARRY. I never met the man before in my life! I swear on Brian May's plectrum!

Scene Five

The First Interview Ever with William Shakespeare

SHAKSPAR. May I just finish this before I go?

BARRY. Do you know any more of my songs?

SHAKSPAR. Yes, but what I like best is that children's book you're working on.

FRANK. You never told me you were working on a children's book.

BARRY. I never told anyone about *Teddy and the Philosopher's Guitar*. What are you, like, a professional mind-reader? Is that your act?

SHAKSPAR. In a way, I suppose I always was, but since I died...

FRANK. Listen, you Shakespeare Kissogram, lookalike fake, bald-headed bladder-faced Midlands Pranny...

BARRY. Hey, Frank, why don't you give him a chance to explain himself.

SHAKSPAR. Because his mind is closed, Barry. He doesn't want to know who wrote the plays. He wants to know he's right. And I think he's probably got some kind of hang-up about common people creating great works of art.

SHAKSPAR *gets up to go.*

BARRY. Now you're talking.

FRANK. No I haven't.

SHAKSPAR. I'm off now. (*Speaking into the camera.*) May I just say thank you to everyone, actors and audiences everywhere, for making my plays the big success they are. I never imagined they would last so long.

FRANK (*also into the camera*). Because he never imagined them in the first place.

SHAKSPAR. I think I might go up to Stratford-upon-Avon and visit the Birthplace Trust. What's the best way to get there?

BARRY. How did you get here?

SHAKSPAR. I don't know... something to do with the internet and the weather? Look, I've written something for you, Frank. Just to show you there's no hard feelings. One of your favourite sonnets. You wouldn't believe the money you can get for any old document connected to me nowadays.

SHAKSPAR *puts it on the desk.*

FRANK. Oh, very impressive. Phoney Elizabethan writing. You've been up all night rehearsing this.

SHAKSPAR. Don't you want a handwritten sonnet?

FRANK. No, I don't want your lousy homework.

> FRANK *tears it up and throws it in his face. Sniffs him.*

> By the way, I don't know if your friends have told you, but you have got severe hygiene issues.

SHAKSPAR. I'll make my own way. Fare thee well, Barry.

BARRY. Fare thee well, Will.

SHAKSPAR. I'm retired; I just want to be left alone, like Prospero. Let your indulgence set me free.

FRANK. If Shakespeare's so like Prospero, why didn't he educate his daughters?

SHAKSPAR. They didn't want to be educated.

FRANK. Why didn't he write or receive any letters?

SHAKSPAR. I conducted my business in person.

FRANK. Why did Shakespeare never write about his home town, Stratford?

SHAKSPAR. Which would you rather go and hear: *The Tragedy of Hamlet, Prince of Denmark*, or *The Slightly Embarrassing Day in the Life of John, Glove Maker of Stratford*?

> *He goes out and they carry on talking around and out in front of the garage.*

FRANK. People in Stratford had no idea he was a playwright?

SHAKSPAR. I kept myself to myself.

FRANK. Then, why was he so litigious?

SHAKSPAR. What's any of this got to do with my work?

FRANK. That's exactly my question.

BARRY. Will, you know you can see inside my head, can you see inside Frank's?

SHAKSPAR. When? In the past, present or future? Once you die, your existence is not bound by time or space.

BARRY. What was Frank doing last Tuesday at, say, 11:37 in the morning?

SHAKSPAR. He was in a classroom, teaching my play, *Romeo and Juliet*, and he was just about to confiscate a mobile telephone from a young student named James who was texting a friend beneath his desk.

BARRY. What did the text say?

FRANK. It doesn't matter.

SHAKSPAR. 'Tosser Charlton is a dickhead.' In the First Folio collection of my plays, Ben Jonson refers to the author as the 'Sweet Swan of Avon'; there's a reference to the author's 'Stratford Monument', in Stratford-upon-Avon; and, my fellow actors, Heminges and Condell, also refer to me as the author. How do you explain all that? Why? If I wasn't the author, why? Until you can answer that, you haven't got an answer, you haven't even got a question!

SHAKSPAR *goes out into the evening.*

Scene Six

Barry and the Crop Circles

BARRY *rushes back inside the garage to address the camera. After a moment,* FRANK *comes back inside as well.*

BARRY. Crop circles!

FRANK. What?

BARRY. Paradigm shifts! Some of the big crop-circle guys in Wiltshire reckon the circles might be communication, from somewhere outside what we are conscious of, via the World Wide Web, the internet. How did Shakespeare say he got here? By the internet!

FRANK. What's that got to do with anything?

BARRY. What if the internet is an incredible communication device, a portal to an astral plane, and with a little help from the lightning, the rain and the wonky wiring in this leaky old garage of yours, it's enabled this guy to travel across space and time?

FRANK. A time machine? That's impossible.

BARRY. The internet is only twenty years old. When man first discovered electricity, he didn't immediately think: 'Hey, I'll have an electric hedge-trimmer.'

[FRANK. Okay, the internet is new, but, Barry – astral planes, time-travel, life after death, none of that's scientific.

BARRY. Flying wasn't scientific once. Only witches did it on broomsticks. Do you know how long it takes the average person to change their mind about a fundamental belief? Twenty-five to forty years!]

Where do you live, Frank? Where are we?

FRANK. 33 Oak Tree Close, Maidstone.

BARRY. No, which galaxy?

FRANK. The Milky Way.

BARRY. Wrong, The Sagittarius Dwarf Galaxy, which scientists have only just discovered is being swallowed by the Milky Way Galaxy – in what part of man's known history has there not been some massive… fucking… thing… he doesn't know anything about… which is just about to wedge open the door of his mind for ever! – Don't you see, for decades you firmly believe you're a citizen of the Milky Way and then one morning – PZHAM! – you're a Sagittarius dwarf.

FRANK. What are you saying?

BARRY. I'm saying we're both Sagittarius dwarfs and that guy wasn't a lookalike. It was him, William Shakespeare himself. How did he know my song? How did he know exactly what you were doing last Tuesday at 11:47 in the morning?

FRANK. How did he know the message on the text?

BARRY.... about *Teddy and the Philosopher's Guitar*?

FRANK.... or all the things he knew. He knew your name.

BARRY. He knew your name.

FRANK.... and my dad's name. He knew me better than my own brother.

BARRY. You haven't got a brother.

FRANK. No, but if I did.

Pause.

Wait a minute. It can't be him. He said he wrote the plays.

BARRY. Exactly. He said he wrote the plays.

FRANK. Oh my God. Maybe you're right, Barry. It was him. Maybe the first guest ever on *Who's There?*, the international Shakespeare authorship show, was the real live author William Shakespeare and...

BARRY. You said he had severe hygiene issues.

FRANK. Oh my God! How could you let me do that, Barry!

BARRY. You were out of control, a man possessed. You tore up his sonnet.

FRANK. I tore up the first authentic handwritten Shakespearean sonnet ever known to mankind.

BARRY. Live on the internet. You're going to be very famous, Frank.

FRANK. Famous?! They'll lynch me.

BARRY *retrieves the fragments of the torn-up sonnet and sticks them together with tape from* FRANK'*s desk*.

BARRY. Don't worry, Frank. I can fix it.

FRANK. When he gets to Stratford, the world's media will want to know where he first appeared, who he spoke to, what I said. Breakfast news. Lunch news. The evening news and then, oh my God. It'll be *Newsnight* and Jeremy Paxman. Paxman loves Shakespeare. They'll set Paxman on me. Oh God! Oh God! Oh God! Paxman's gonna eat me alive!

BARRY. Don't worry, you're going to be all right. I know how to deal with the media. I've been reading the Alastair Campbell diaries. Focus the camera and sit down in that seat. I'll pretend to be Alastair Campbell pretending to be Jeremy Paxman and you pretend to be you.

FRANK. Are you sure?

BARRY. Trust me, Frank.

They sit, as if doing a Newsnight *interview.* BARRY *turns down the lights and plays some appropriate* Newsnight-*type music on the Korg by remote control.*

(With thick Scottish accent.) So, Mr Charlton, did you or did you not...

FRANK. Barry, Jeremy Paxman isn't Scottish.

BARRY. Nevertheless... did you or did you not tear up the first authentic handwritten Shakespearean sonnet ever known to mankind and throw it in the face of William Shakespeare?

FRANK. I... I... I... I... I...

BARRY. Did you or didn't you, Mr Charlton?

FRANK. Well, I, you see... I'd had a bad day and I wasn't sure if...

BARRY. Answer the question!

FRANK. I didn't think he was...

BARRY. Answer the question!

FRANK. I don't know how to answer that question, Barry!

BARRY *hands* FRANK *the reconstituted sonnet, and demonstrates what* FRANK *should say.*

BARRY *(with a Scottish accent)*. 'Ah well, that's where you're wrong, Jeremy.'

FRANK. Barry, I don't have a Scottish accent.

BARRY *(without a Scottish accent)*. 'I didn't tear up the sonnet because I have it here, covered in a protective coat of Sellotape.

(*As Paxman again.*) Then read it out to us and prove you are innocent?

FRANK (*reading*).
     'Shall I summer thee to a compare day?
     May darling, have you untrimmed your rough buds?
     Lovely…'

Barry! That's utter rubbish!

BARRY. It could work.

FRANK. No. It's a disaster.

Realising with horror.

And it's all gone out live on the internet. I'm finished.

Scene Seven

Shakespeare's Triumphant Return

SHAKSPAR. Are we still live on the internet?

SHAKSPAR *appears again at the back door.*

BARRY. Yes.

SHAKSPAR. Good. Don't log off. I walked about fifty feet down your lane, just past The Coach and Horses, and my hands disappeared. I think I might have a very limited range.

BARRY. He's back! Great to have you back! Welcome to the *Astral Authorship Spaceship Show*!

FRANK. Here, Barry, record it with this tape.

Handing BARRY *a tape.*

BARRY. You are not going to record over *Spartacus*.

FRANK. What are you talking about, Barry? It's William Shakespeare!

BARRY. Okay, okay. Walk into shot, Will. That's how they do it.

> BARRY *plays chat-show introductory walk-down music.* FRANK *clears the desk and puts his suit jacket on.* BARRY *presses the ecstatic applause button.*

> Yeah, come down here, out of camera shot, and then walk in, shake his hand and sit down. And we're off.

> Go camera one.

FRANK. Welcome to the show, Mr Shakespeare. Please have a seat. I want to begin by apologising to this sweet-natured, gentle genius beside me. What do these men behind me have in common? Who are they? A bunch of fucking idiots. I should know, I was one of them. Oh my God, I haven't even told you how much I love your work. I mean, what can I say, I'm speechless. Harold Bloom was right, your incredible mind… I mean, you created our concept of a human being…

BARRY. Yeah. I don't get it. I mean Frank's been going on and on about what an idiot you were. How you couldn't have got an education in Stratford because everyone was so stupid there. Your dad was so dim couldn't sign his name. Stupid. Everyone was thick. That's the picture he's painted.

> [*For some reason I have made a note here that says:* 'phone call'. *I think I might mean that if we wanted to have one arranged call, to encourage a shy audience, we would place it here in the previous speech as it can be interrupted by a call, and then* BARRY *can pick up the scene again in the middle of the speech. Worth a try! Hopefully you won't need to encourage, quite the opposite.*]

FRANK. Thank you, Barry, for your opinions. Do you have a question for our special guest?

BARRY. Where did you get your education?

SHAKSPAR. I attended the King's Free Grammar School of Stratford-upon-Avon. My father was an alderman; it was my right.

FRANK. Have you got any more stupid questions, Barry?

SHAKSPAR. No, I understand Barry's question. The school records of those years, when I attended, have been lost, so you have no proof I ever attended any educational institution in my entire life.

FRANK. But it's your name on the plays, Will! They prove you were educated. Where else would you have got your education?

SHAKSPAR. Yes, well, some people think that the proven education in my plays and the unproven education in my life, prove that I didn't write the plays.

[FRANK. Prove it. It's the name on the plays.

SHAKSPAR. It's the name *in* the plays.

FRANK. What?

SHAKSPAR. What's the name of the boy student in the Latin grammar lesson in *The Merry Wives of Windsor*?

FRANK. William!

BARRY *presses SFX – 'one hundred and eighty!'– the sound of a commentator at a darts championship announcing the top score.*

SHAKSPAR. Where does the schoolmaster in that play, Sir Hugh Evans, come from?

FRANK. Wales! Wales?

SHAKSPAR. My schoolmaster in Stratford was a Welshman.

BARRY *presses SFX – 'one hundred and eighty!'* BARRY *and* FRANK *sing a bit of a Welsh song.*]

FRANK. Well, some people say an aristocrat had to have written these plays.

SHAKSPAR. It's true people think, because I wrote in a style to please aristocrats, that one of the aristocrats must have written the plays!

FRANK. That's very funny. [Or: 'Cor Blimey!']

SHAKSPAR. I wrote what pleased them, and what reflected them pleased them. I held a mirror up to their nature. People think all writing is personal since the Romantic age of Byron, Shelley, Keats, where people bared their souls in what they wrote, but in my time it wasn't personal.

FRANK. It wasn't about personal revelation.

SHAKSPAR. It was about making a living…

FRANK. Making a living! By the way, what were they thinking, Will? What were people thinking when you died? How come not a single person, your friends, your acting mates at the Globe, no one from the whole world of literature and theatre in 1616, says a single word? When your colleague, the actor Richard Burbage died, people are reported to have run out of their houses and wept in the streets.

SHAKSPAR. What's your favourite film?

FRANK. I don't know. I don't have a single favourite. I recorded *Spartacus* last night. That's a fantastic film.

SHAKSPAR. Who's your favourite actor in it?

FRANK. Laurence Olivier's pretty brilliant…

SHAKSPAR. Was there a fuss when he died?

FRANK. You bet there was. Westminster Abbey.

SHAKSPAR. Who wrote *Spartacus*?

FRANK. I don't know.

BARRY *plays his victory sound effect again.*

SHAKSPAR. Frank, could I ask a favour?

FRANK. Anything. Anything, Will.

SHAKSPAR. Would you mind if I go and help myself to a beer?

FRANK. You go right ahead, Will. They're in my house, in the refrigerator, in the kitchen.

BARRY. Will, I'd just like to say, I am learning so much tonight. If I hadn't met you in the flesh, I never would have known that William Shakespeare had such massive thighs.

SHAKSPAR. Thank you, Barry.

BARRY. Do you want me to fetch you a beer?

SHAKSPAR. Really, that's all right, Barry, thanks.

FRANK. He can do it by himself, Barry. By himself, like he wrote the plays.

SHAKSPAR *exits*.

Scene Eight

From Limits Far Remote

FRANK *and* BARRY *celebrate and then* FRANK *suddenly stops*.

BARRY. You were right. He stinks like a farmyard, but he's a fucking genius. Wait till I call the Wiltshire crop-circle guys!

FRANK. Yeah, wait till I tell all the professors up at the Shakespeare Institute...

BARRY. What is it?

FRANK. You don't understand, Barry, I was wrong about Shakespeare. You were right about crop circles being communication from an astral plane, but all these years I've been wrong. William Shakespeare did write Shakespeare.

BARRY. How were you to know?

FRANK. It's got his name on it.

BARRY. Well, it's an easy mistake to make. So, you were wrong about crop circles too. It doesn't matter if you can admit it.

FRANK. Yeah, do you think it's all right? If you admit it. If you say you're sorry. Oh, Barry, you are like the best friend I ever... You know those crop-circle books you lent me once? Can I borrow them again, and this time, read them?

BARRY. Of course. You know *The Complete Works of Shakespeare* you're always telling me to read?

FRANK. Yes.

BARRY. Can I borrow your lawnmower?

FRANK. Course. Barry, he appeared in a garage, my obscure little garage in Maidstone. Why?

BARRY. Don't take this wrong, Frank, but you are a couple of plays short of a full folio.

FRANK. Eh?

BARRY. I mean, who thinks about Shakespeare as much as you? Your thought entered the world brain of the internet, the universal search engine, and made him appear here… like a Tudor email. Your thoughts drew him here. Across huge distances of time and space.

BACON *walks up the driveway and through the (invisible) closed garage door into the garage as* FRANK *recalls a sonnet.*

FRANK. Thinking makes it so. Listen to this:

'If the dull substance of my flesh were thought,
Injurious distance should not stop my way,
For then despite of space I would be brought,
From limits far remote, where thou dost stay…'

BARRY. Hey, I just thought of some song lyrics.

Going to the Korg as BACON *also speaks the sonnet.*

'No matter then although my foot did stand,
Upon the farthest earth removed from thee,
For nimble thought can jump both sea and land,
As soon as think the place where he would be.'

What d'you think of that?

FRANK. That's the rest of the sonnet… the next stanza.

BARRY. Fuck off. I just made it up.

FRANK. No, you didn't. I just spoke the first stanza of sonnet number 44 and then you spoke the next. Perfect.

BARRY. Did I? Where'd that come from?

FRANK. I don't know.

BACON. I do.

BACON *materialises in front of them.*

Scene Nine

The Second Guest Ever: Sir Francis Bacon

BACON. By far the greatest obstacle to the progress of science, and to the understanding of new tastes and provinces therein, is found in this: that men despair and think things impossible. The internet, Barry.

BARRY. It's another one, Frank!

BACON. Mr Charlton, I'm a great admirer of inductive reasoning, if you would indulge me for only a few minutes, while Mr Shakspeare explores your refrigerator – what a sublime invention that is – I would very much like to assist your inquisition.

BARRY. And this one didn't even use the door.

BACON. Yes, Barry. I had no idea when I discovered the binary code, the root of the computer, such things would be possible. But then polarity – strife and friendship – is at the root of everything. Your age has created a world mind with all the potential capabilities of an individual mind.

BARRY. That's what I was saying. Only he said it a lot better.

BACON. What you call inspiration, intuition, is really thought arriving in your individual mind from outside your self. Like an intuition, I have arrived in your world mind from an astral plane of pure thought, of nothing. Barry is absolutely right. A natural genius.

FRANK. Barry's a natural genius?

BARRY. I like this guy. Who is he?

FRANK. It's Sir Francis Bacon. Viscount St Albans. The Baron Verulam. One of the most powerful and influential figures of Shakespeare's time.

BARRY. Never heard of him.

BACON. As I wrote, the monuments of wit and learning are more durable than the monuments of power.

FRANK.
'Not marble nor the gilded monuments of princes,
Shall outlive this powerful rhyme…'

BACON. Well said. You know your Shakespeare.

FRANK. I do. You know your Bacon.

BACON. I am.

BARRY. You both know your onions.

FRANK. I can't believe it.

BACON. You are believing it.

FRANK. Did you write Shakespeare?

BARRY. Frank.

BACON. I despise idolatry, Frank. I always have. Idols of the mind. Idols of the theatre.

BARRY. *Pop Idol*?

BACON. This idolatry of the man from Stratford is obstructing the understanding of the plays. People should fall in love with the teaching, not the teacher.

FRANK. How does the idolatry of a natural-born genius present any obstacle to what might be in the plays?

BACON. An all-knowing, natural-born genius wasn't an obstacle. Modern scholarship, however, has discovered an ill-educated, bookless actor of dubious financial dealings and ardent Catholicism and now must make the plays fit that man's rather limited mind. This is what concerns me.

FRANK. Yes, yes, yes. So you wrote the works of Shakespeare?

BARRY. Frank.

BACON. Ah, the mystery of identity. Do you know, Frank, from the perspective of an atom there is no difference between you and that lawnmower?

BARRY. Frank, come here. What about the man in the kitchen?

FRANK. I know, but Bacon's got all the education and almost all the life experience that's in the plays. He's one of the strongest candidates. He told a friend he was a concealed poet, Barry. Secret.

BACON. If you couldn't keep a secret in my time, you lost your head. We kept much larger secrets than who wrote plays.

BARRY. Why would anyone want to keep it secret if they wrote Shakespeare?

BACON. We lived in an iron and malicious age of privilege, Barry, a vicious tyranny of wealthy families. Nowadays, you don't realise the political sensitivity of the Shakespeare plays. Poor John Stubbes. Do you recall his misfortune, Frank?

FRANK. A single line of Stubbes' writing was thought to contain an implicit criticism of Queen Elizabeth. He denied that he had meant any such thing. The authorities said it didn't matter whether he meant it or not and cut his hand off.

BARRY. Stubbes by name, Stubbes by nature.

BACON. There were many notable men at court who suppressed their poetry or published under another's name. Especially love poetry. A poem like *Venus and Adonis* was considered pornographic...

BARRY. Venus and who?

BARRY *attempts to write it down.*

FRANK. *Venus and Adonis*. It's the first work with the name Shakespeare on it and only a few years after it was published, two poets, Hall and Marston, point to Bacon as the author.

BARRY. You wrote porn?

FRANK. It's not porn, Barry.

BACON. To write for the public theatres would have been like your Prince Charles putting himself on *Big Brother*.

FRANK. But you're the father of modern science, why would a scientist write plays?

BACON. Why did da Vinci, the inventor of the tank, paint the *Mona Lisa*? My primary scientific concern was the human state, the human heart and mind and spirit. Do you know I considered publishing all my known works under pseudonyms? I so loved secrecy, codes and masks.

FRANK. Did you write the works of Shakespeare?

BARRY. Shakespeare said he did it. It's his name on the plays.

BACON. The Shakespeare works are designed to mirror nature, and nature's author is always hidden. She wears a mask of nature. Was Shakespeare really his name?

BARRY. What does he mean?

FRANK. Oh, Shakspar. When the Stratford man signs his name he writes Shakspar…

BARRY. Shakes*peare*, Frank. Not Spar, that's a little supermarket.

FRANK. You don't understand, Barry. Look!

FRANK *shows signatures and frontispieces to* BARRY *on the screen. They appear on the screens above as well.*

When the actor signs his name – these six signatures are the only examples of his handwriting we have –

BARRY. He has got terrible handwriting.

FRANK. Yes, how could people read his manuscripts? But you see he writes Shakspar, or Shagspere, Shakspere, never Shakespeare or Shake-hyphen-speare. Did you choose the actor William Shakspar as a front for the plays of Shakespeare?

BACON. Did you know, Barry, that Pallas Athena literally means the spear-shaker: Pallas Athena, the Greek Goddess of Wisdom, brandishing her spear at the eyes of ignorance. Shaking her spear, sending a vibrating sound, word, an idea in our consciousness. You ask, 'Who chose Shakspar as a front?' What force in the universe chooses any artist as a front for inspiration? Where do your songs come from, Barry?

BARRY. I was inspired with a song tonight. Completely out of the blue.

BACON. Oh, then I see Queen Mab hath been with you.

BARRY. Could be. The eighties are such a blur.

[*I have a note to self here: 'Advert from* FRANK *to ring the show.' Make of it what you will.*]

So you're telling me this guy in the kitchen is a front?

BACON. Sometimes I'm amazed that our front has survived as long as he has. In our time, the silence about him as a writer was deafening, don't you find, Frank?

FRANK. Yes, even his contemporary theatre managers, Henslowe and Alleyne, don't mention Shakespeare once in their diaries and account books, despite their many references to other playwrights and theatre people. They even purchase for staging the plays *King Lear* and *Hamlet* without mention of Shakespeare. Henslowe actually paid two other men for *Troilus and Cressida*.

[BACON. A few more discoveries like those diaries, and the mask will drop.

FRANK. Do you think there will be more discoveries?

BACON. Most certainly, if they are accepted as discoveries. What happened to that mural in St Albans?

FRANK. They covered it up. A late-sixteenth-century mural, discovered in 1985, depicting erotic scenes from *Venus and Adonis*...

BARRY. That love poem.

FRANK. Yes… dismissed as unimportant by Stratfordians. A large part of it has never even been revealed.

BARRY. That's sometimes a good thing. More sexy that way.

FRANK. That's not the reason. It's because it was found in the nearest inn to his house, outside St Albans.

BACON. Would that have been the case if it had been discovered in Stratford?

FRANK. No.]

BARRY. All right, if Shakespeare is a front, why back Bacon?

FRANK. Why back Bacon? What about the inventory of the Northumberland Manuscript, Sir Francis?

FRANK *shows close-ups of the Northumberland Manuscript to* BARRY *on the screen. They appear on the screens above as well.*

Look at this, Barry! In the late-nineteenth century, a bundle of Elizabethan papers belonging to Francis Bacon was discovered at Northumberland House on the Strand in London. The bundle was wrapped in a cover and on the cover was an inventory of its contents, including the titles of two plays *Richard II* and *Richard III*. This is the earliest known reference to a Shakespearean manuscript. Now, the name of William Shakespeare appears sixteen times at the bottom of the manuscript, as if someone is practising it…

BARRY. Well, this is an own goal. It's got his name on it.

FRANK. Wait a minute, Barry. Look, the scribe never puts the word 'by' before Shakespeare. Look, to the left of the title *Richard II* are the words 'by Mr Francis Bacon'. Can you see that?

BARRY. That's incredible.

FRANK. Why are you the first person in history to possess a bundle with the names Shakespeare and Bacon all over it, which contained original manuscripts of two plays that had not yet been published under Shakespeare's name?

BACON. Good question.

BARRY. Why have I never heard of this bundle?

FRANK. Yes, exactly. Any equivalent manuscript bundle that
had on it the words 'by William Shakspar', would be the
central piece of evidence for Mr Shakspar's case.

BACON. It would be a unique and priceless artefact, but my
cousin Sir Henry Neville's name appears on the manuscript –
he's an authorship candidate – and my brother Anthony's as
well.

FRANK. Don't you want to prove you wrote the plays?

BACON. No, that is not my intention.

FRANK. Not your intention! For God's sake, you've been the
prime suspect for two hundred years. You even wrote that
you were going to create something like the Shakespeare
plays. Why? Why? Why didn't you leave some irrefutable
evidence that you did in fact write the works of
Shakespeare? I lost my job because of your bloody secrecy.

BARRY. He lost more than that.

BACON. By the way, have you lost Shakspeare?

FRANK. Oh my God.

BARRY. He's in your kitchen fetching a beer.

BACON. Have you still got a live webcam in your refrigerator?

FRANK. Yes. That one you put in there last Christmas.

They tune into the fridge webcam and we see SHAKSPAR
*looking into the fridge in big close-up. We see him pick up
something and look at it.*

He's eating my breakfast.

FRANK *goes to an intercom panel on the desk, and speaks
into the microphone.*

Hey, Will! Put the bacon back. There's ham on the bottom
shelf. Don't nick the bacon.

BACON. Let me go and fetch our friend William. I'll be right
back. I'm dying to see this refrigerator.

BACON *exits swiftly and gracefully through the back door.*

Scene Ten

One of Them's a Liar

FRANK. Why won't he say it? He's hiding. He's playing with us. It's a game of cat and mouse.

BARRY. Yeah, but who's the cat and who's the mouse? I mean, it's got to be the man from Stratford. They've got his birthplace and Anne Hathaway's cottage. I went there once on Mrs Somerville's school trip. I got an ice cream from 'As You Lick It'.

FRANK. Shakespeare's birthplace is a sham!

BARRY. Shakespeare's birthplace, a sham? You can't say that. Mrs Somerville cried when she showed us Shakespeare's birthplace. I bought a leather comb-case and a packet of Shakespeare mints.

FRANK. You were conned. It's all built on nothing, a vacuum. There's no evidence that Shakspar's father occupied a house on Henley Street when Shakspar was born.

BARRY. You mean to tell me that my whole school trip was a rip-off? I'm going to have them for false advertising under the Trade Descriptions Act.

FRANK. It's been done. Francis Carr. 1969. He lost the case. It didn't apply – the Stratford magistrates ruled – because the Stratford tourist trade isn't a business, it's a Trust. The Birthplace Trust. And that's all it is, trust.

BARRY. I don't know about all this, Frank. What are you going to gain?

FRANK. How can we know who we are, if we don't know where we came from? In Stratford, young people get the impression that great art, like Shakespeare, is pulled out of thin air, just dreamt up like magic, without any education or life experience. Great art is not a fantasy. It's based on observation of what's actually happening in the world around you. Think what a horrible demon Shakespeare is to so many young writers, because his life story makes them think writing is a kind of creationalist miracle.

BARRY. But as soon as you prove that someone else wrote Shakespeare, then the 'As You Lick It', the MacDonald's, the whole ShakExperience thing you hate, just packs up and trucks over to the new guy's birthplace, and the whole thing starts up again.

FRANK. No, it won't be the same. Francis Bacon has a life story. It's because of the vacuum of Shakspar's life story that all that corporate rubbish has taken hold in Stratford-upon Avon. There's nothing there. The birthplace, Anne Hathaway's cottage, even the bust in Trinity Church, they're all a sham.

BARRY. Well, maybe they did it together. Bacon and Shakespeare. Maybe they were best friends. Look! Their names are together on that manuscript. Pen pals!

FRANK. Yeah, but why hide it? Bacon and the author of the Shakespeare works stand together as the two writers of exceptional genius in their time, yet search every other document we have and they never mention each other. Why?

BARRY. Two guys standing together like that and never talking. Are you sure?

FRANK. Yes. They never acknowledge each other.

BARRY. That is weird.

FRANK. While still a teenager at Cambridge University, Bacon launched his Great Instauration.

BARRY. His what?

FRANK. His worldwide regeneration of all learning, insisting that learning should be enjoyable and come from direct observation of nature.

BARRY. Wait a minute – did Shakespeare like to get close to nature too?

FRANK. Yes, the plays are full of observations of nature. Human nature as well as the natural world.

BARRY. Mountains?

FRANK. Yes, mountains, everything, the open air, the bottom of the sea, plants, animals, but mostly human nature.

BARRY. Animals, like horses?

FRANK. Certainly, lots of horses. 'My kingdom for a horse!' But Bacon's prime interest was the interplay of man's passion, to be demonstrated by historical drama and fable.

BARRY. I've got it! They were secret lovers. Elizabethan cowboys. You know, like in *Brokeback Mountain* and first they tried to fight it, deny it, but then they couldn't help each other, it was bigger than both of them, and so they tried to hide it from everyone else by standing together as geniuses at great installations, ignoring each other and acting tough even though deep down they just wanted to kiss and cuddle each other and go out riding bareback into nature, and dress up and do plays in the open air about fairies and bottoms. What are they doing now? In the film, they couldn't help embracing and having a kiss whenever they were alone. Maybe we'll catch them at it and one of the great literary conundrums will be solved.

BARRY *looks on the computer at the kitchen webcam. We see what he sees,* BACON *with his hand up a frozen chicken.*

What on earth is he doing?

FRANK. He's testing how cold it is. Francis Bacon died of pneumonia after conducting an early experiment in refrigeration by stuffing snow up a chicken.

BARRY. They're coming back.

FRANK. We've nearly got it. We're nearly there. If Shakspar wrote, they both wrote such similar things, there can only be two possibilities: either Shakspar is a genius and Bacon's his advisor, or Bacon is a genius and Shakspar's just his front. They have to have been involved with each other. They have to have known each other intimately.

BARRY. Intimately.

FRANK. Don't worry. I've been in this situation before at school many times during exams. You sometimes get two boys submitting papers that are almost identical to each other. It's called cheating. You have to call them in after school and have it out with them.

BACON *and* SHAKSPAR *return from the kitchen.*

Scene Eleven

Bacon and Shakspar, Together at Last!

BACON *and* SHAKSPAR *re-enter, laughing and talking about frozen chicken and beer.*

BACON. That chicken, Frank, my hand is still tingling. Could we defrost it and roast it later for dinner? I would be fascinated to know if the taste is altered.

SHAKSPAR. If it tastes anything like this beer it won't taste like chicken at all. Nothing tastes like itself any more, Francis. Here, hold this and chase me. Oh, oh, exit pursued by a beer!

FRANK. So you two know each other then?

SHAKSPAR. Never met before in our lives, but it's been like meeting a brother!

BACON. I can't believe how much we share.

FRANK. Never met before in your lives? Well, come in and sit down. We don't want to keep you very long. You see, Barry and I have a little problem and we need your help.

BARRY. But first we want to encourage you to relax and be yourselves. You can tell us.

FRANK. We understand.

BARRY. You'll feel better if you get it off your chest.

FRANK. Tell us the truth. You've borne the secret of your relationship for three hundred and ninety years.

BARRY. Just come out and say it.

FRANK. Thanks, Barry. I'll handle this. Now, as an English teacher, I've a keen eye for writing, and from what I know of the writing work you two have submitted in your names, I can safely say that you stand together as the towering geniuses of your generation. The top of your class. A-plus. Well done. You can relax about that. There's no problem there.

BARRY. We have no problem with you standing together.

FRANK. Have you ever heard of a parallelism, gentlemen?

It's a correspondence between the writing of two authors. It may be a thought that is shared, or language, or both. For example, William, it's how we know that sometimes you collaborated with other writers. *Pericles*, for example, *Macbeth*. Two thirds of your fellow writers for the theatre wrote collaboratively. I have here some examples of your writing, boys. These are from your wonderful plays, William. And these are from your notebook, your storehouse of phrases you heard which you collected for later use, Francis.

FRANK *drops a cloth behind his desk with a selection of parallelisms.* *

There are one thousand, one hundred parallelisms to be found between your writing, boys. Six hundred of those parallelisms can be found in Francis's private notebook alone! That is called cheating, boys. Copying.

BARRY. What have you been sharing?

FRANK. We want to know who is relying on who?

BARRY. Who is lying on who?

FRANK. Who is copying who?

BARRY. Did you do it together?

FRANK. How could the two of you *not* have been involved with each other? You had to have done it together. We know you had to have been together at the first performance of *A*

---

* See page 98 for examples of parallelisms between Bacon and Shakespeare.

Comedy of Errors! Ben Jonson described you both wearing the theatrical socks of comedy and bettering all that insolent Greece or haughty Rome sent forth. The same words for both of you.

BARRY. Naughty Rome!

FRANK. We know Ben Jonson loved you both.

BARRY. Was it a threesome?

OXFORD *kicks down the door.*

Scene Twelve

The Third Guest Ever: Edward de Vere

There is a loud crash as EDWARD DE VERE, *the* EARL OF OXFORD, *kicks the back door open and enters sword in hand.*

OXFORD (*considers himself in the flesh again*). What a piece of work is a man! How noble in reason, how infinite in faculty, in form and moving how express and admirable, in action how like an angel, in apprehension how like a God the beauty of the world, the paragon of animals! And yet to me what is this quintessence of dust? Man delights not me – nor woman neither…

BARRY. Time out, D'Artagnon! I don't know about where you come from but where I live, here in Maidstone – it's all right, Frank, I'll deal with this – you usually knock before smashing your way into a room. Knock, knock. Who's there?

OXFORD *puts his sword to* BARRY's *throat.*

OXFORD. Oh, know my name is lost, fool. Report me and my cause aright to the unsatisfied, Charlton. Report me and my cause aright. I hereby proclaim that I, Edward de Vere, the seventeenth Earl of Oxford, am William Shakespeare.

FRANK. My Lord Oxford, there's no need to threaten my friend.

BARRY. It's all right, Frank, he's just a ghost. Ghosts can't hurt you.

OXFORD *slices the head off the teddy with his sword.*
BARRY *kneels on the floor and cradles the headless teddy and head.*

Alas, poor teddy.

OXFORD. You entertain fools too readily, Charlton. Mr Bacon, how strange to see you, my little cousin, older than myself. A knight to boot, a lord.

BACON. Yes, cousin. All after your death, from the hand of our gracious King James.

OXFORD. 'Mediocria Firma.' Your middle way proved a profitable one in the eyes of that Scotsman.

BACON. I served my king as faithfully as I could.

OXFORD. Would you have served me, cousin, as your king?

BACON. That situation never arose.

OXFORD. What makes a king, Charlton? A real king? Is it blood? Is it self-mastery? What makes a king a king? What was a drama for others, was my life. Charlton, these works aren't some conscious scheme, some toy in the Great Instauration of society. They are certainly not some actor-manager's playhouse pension plan. They are an unconscious cry from the heart. I pulled them kicking and screaming from the deepest pits of my darkest hours. That's why they have their power, their passion, their monstrous indiscretion.

SHAKSPAR. Frank, no one denies Lord Oxford's tormented, outcast life, but any connection to the plays is pure conjecture. The baseless fantasy of pseudo-psychologists.

OXFORD. Pseudo-psychologists? Dr Sigmund Freud. I quote, 'The man from Stratford seems to have nothing at all to justify his claim, whereas Oxford has almost everything.'

SHAKSPAR. Do you really believe Hamlet de Vere wrote all my plays because he wanted to murder his father and sleep with his mother? Which day in his life did he meet the Merry Wives of Windsor?

BACON. There are more things in heaven and earth, my lord, than the Oedipus complex.

OXFORD. The voice of Hamlet cries out through all the plays. It is the most important character in the central play of the entire works. What possible connection can you determine between your lives and the life of Hamlet? My life is so similar, you would do better to claim you were writing it about me, but you don't dare invite the comparison. These plays were born in my life, Charlton. I wrote to heal the wounds of my soul and in that healing touched upon the wounds of the world soul.

SHAKSPAR. This is all just an elaborate defence mechanism to glorify their ignominious and forgotten lives.

OXFORD. You social-climbing little snob.

BARRY. Shall we order in tonight, Frank, just for a change?

SHAKSPAR. You're just a bunch of disenfranchised imperialists… out of a job… with rotten stinking reputations… stealing the natural gifts of the common man.

BARRY. Anyone for a Thai takeaway?

BACON. There is but one case wherein a man may commend himself with good grace, and that is in commending virtue in another.

SHAKSPAR. You and your great enlightenment of society… one rotten poem about a bubble and a scientific materialism that is destroying the nature you claim to love, as we speak. Atheists! Necromancers! Pederasts! The both of you. Is that who you think wrote Shakespeare, Frank… a couple of pederasts?

BARRY. A cup of tea?

OXFORD. How dare you accuse me of pederasty! You little upstart crow. Captain Pod. If only they'd killed you rather than Marlowe. You've basked in the hard graft of my suffering existence… born of the kind of pain you never experienced in your nasty little life, hoarding grain from your beloved fellow common man in time of famine… attempting to enclose common lands around Stratford…

leaving your long-suffering wife to borrow shillings from a servant... a debt you never repaid... you tight-fisted little nouveau riche tax-dodger...

SHAKSPAR. My long-suffering wife. That's rich. That's rich coming from you. What about Anne Cecil, his innocent teenage wife, abandoned for five years while he shagged Italian altar boys in Venice?

OXFORD. Hamnet Shakspar, his innocent little boy, died in poverty, his mother begging servants for shillings, while his father flaunted it in London on the riches I paid you to front my plays.

SHAKSPAR. The Devil take thy soul!

OXFORD. I loved Anne Cecil; forty thousand brothers with all their quantity of love could not make up my sum!

OXFORD *grabs* SHAKSPAR *by the throat.* FRANK *accidentally falls on the keyboard, setting off a loud Shakespeare film soundtrack.*

SHAKSPAR. I prithee, take thy fingers from my throat!

OXFORD. Away thy hand!

FRANK. Pull them apart!

BARRY. Fellas!

BACON. Good my lord, be quiet!

OXFORD.
 Why, I will fight with him upon this theme
 Until my eyelids will no longer wag.

BACON (*underneath the following dialogue*). Revenge is a kind of wild justice, gentlemen... in passing it over, you are far superior... it is a prince's part to pardon, my lord... That which is past is gone, and irrevocable... Wise men have enough to do with things present and to come... You but trifle with yourselves to labour in past matters.

BARRY. Oh, he's mad, Frank.

FRANK. For love of God, let him go, Will.

SHAKSPAR. Nay, an thou'lt mouth my lines, I'll rant as well as thou!

OXFORD.
Swounds, show me what thou'lt do.
Woot weep?

SHAKSPAR.
woot fight?

OXFORD.
woot fast?

SHAKSPAR.
woot tear thyself?

OXFORD.
Woot drink up eisel?

SHAKSPAR.
eat a crocodile?

OXFORD *and* SHAKSPAR.
I'll do it.

SHAKSPAR.
Does thou come here to whine?
To outface me with leaping in my grave?

OXFORD.
This is I,
Hamlet the Dane.

OXFORD *frees himself and draws his sword.*

SERGEANT FREEMAN *of the Kent County Constabulary enters through the back door.*

SERGEANT. Mid Kent Constabulary! Nobody move!

Now, who the hell do you lot think you are?

Blackout.

End of Act One.

ACT TWO

Scene One

The Policeman, the Ripper and the Earl

Lights up. There has obviously been a struggle. The
SERGEANT *has disarmed* OXFORD *and handcuffed him to
the lawnmower. All else, bar the* SERGEANT, *are prone on the
floor.*

SERGEANT. You do not have to say anything, but it may harm
your defence if you do not mention when questioned
something which you later rely on in court. Anything you do
say may be given in evidence. Do you understand?

OXFORD *nods. The* SERGEANT *gets out his notepad.*

FRANK *turns the television to the wall so that the*
SERGEANT *can't see the camera is on.*

Good. Now, what's going on here? Who's the owner of this
property?

FRANK. I am, sergeant.

Standing.

SERGEANT. Sit down! And your name is?

FRANK. Frank Charlton. I can explain everything, officer. You
see, I'm an English teacher and these friends of mine and I
are preparing a little play about... it's a sort of whodunnit...

SERGEANT. Whodunnit?

FRANK. Yes. We were all just acting.

BARRY. Frank.

FRANK. Yes?

BARRY. Is this a play?

FRANK. Yes… you remember…

BARRY. No.

FRANK. Yes. We're acting in a play.

BARRY. Am I in it?

FRANK. Umm… Yes, you play the neighbour.

SERGEANT. What's this whodunnit about then?

FRANK. It's about William Shakespeare.

SERGEANT. What's your name?

SHAKSPAR. William Shakespeare.

SERGEANT. You?

BACON. Francis Bacon.

SERGEANT. Yes?

Pointing to BARRY.

BARRY. Barry Wild.

SERGEANT (*with suspicion*). Barry Wild?

BARRY. Yes.

SERGEANT. So you're practising a play?

FRANK. Yes, you see. No one was really upset. We were just acting.

SERGEANT. Ed, here, seemed pretty upset. Was he just acting when he attacked me?

FRANK. Well, he got confused… because… we're waiting for one of our actors to arrive, you see, who was going to play a uniformed policeman, and he thought you were that actor.

SERGEANT. One of your actors was going to impersonate a policeman?

FRANK. Yes.

SERGEANT. Have you got a licence for that, Charlton?

FRANK. No, sergeant.

SERGEANT. Well, you better get one. There are very strict rules about impersonating policemen in plays.

FRANK. Yes, sergeant. My point was that he didn't mean to attack you. He's what you call a method actor. Takes it all very personally. Finds it difficult sometimes to see the difference between his own life and the play.

OXFORD. It is my life, Charlton. Were they robbed by pirates on the English Channel, stripped and left naked on the shores of England like Hamlet? I was.

SHAKSPAR. Theatre is not always about personal revelation. I thought you agreed with me, Frank?

SERGEANT. All right, calm down. It's just a play after all. I'm afraid I'm going to have to take him down to the station and confiscate this weapon.

FRANK. Do you really have to take him down to the station?

SERGEANT. Yes.

BARRY. Sergeant, earlier on, when Will went past The Coach and Horses, his hands disappeared. Those cuffs are gonna slip straight off.

SERGEANT. What?

FRANK. Yes. That's right, Barry. That's your line in the play, but wait till I give you a cue to speak. Remember, don't speak, don't say anything, before I give you the cue.

OXFORD *becomes quite agitated*.

SERGEANT. You had better tell your friend to calm down. I don't want to have to call over a van.

SHAKSPAR. He's a dangerous man, sergeant. He murdered a servingman once.

FRANK. In the play, in the play, not in real life. Let's all calm down.

BACON. Would you like a cup of tea, sergeant? Perhaps if you give your prisoner a few minutes to calm down he will become more manageable.

SERGEANT. Well…

FRANK. Yes. It's the least we can do for causing you this trouble. Barry, get him a cup of tea.

BARRY. Really? Or is this in the play?

FRANK. Both.

BACON. May I try a cup of tea?

BARRY. Milk, sugar? One or two?

SERGEANT. Milk, two sugars.

BACON. Is that the ideal way to take tea?

SERGEANT. I like it that way.

BACON. I'll have the same as the sergeant, but no milk.

BARRY. Anyone else?

SHAKSPAR. What's tea like?

FRANK. Why don't you have a small beer, Will.

OXFORD. Sack, Spanish sack if you have it, with some sugar.

BARRY. What do I say now, Frank? In the play?

FRANK. Just get out, Barry. Get some drinks.

BARRY. Just get out, Barry. Get some drinks.

BARRY *goes out.*

SERGEANT. I never went in for acting myself, but my brother is a great enthusiast, you know, in an amateur fashion. Oh yes, he's the clever one. Always was. Loves his Shakespeare. So what's all this arguing and upsetting the neighbours with your play?

FRANK. Are the neighbours upset?

SERGEANT. What were you arguing about?

FRANK. The question of who wrote Shakespeare.

SERGEANT. Oh, right, Jack the Ripper.

FRANK. You think Jack the Ripper wrote the works of Shakespeare?

SERGEANT. Don't get cocky, sunshine. No, the Shakespeare authorship question always reminds me of Jack the Ripper.

FRANK. Why?

OXFORD. Because Shakespeare lives deep in our dark unconscious fears and doubts about who we really are.

SERGEANT. No, Rambo, because I've heard the authorship question mentioned by colleagues of mine studying the Ripper case.

FRANK. Why did your colleagues mention it?

SERGEANT. The Victorian Ripper diary. The name on the diary is James Maybrick, a Liverpool cotton merchant, but was he actually the killer? Now there's a whodunnit! Who actually wrote it? CBCA.

Starts writing on the whiteboard.

Have you read Professor David Canter, the criminal psychologist, on CBCA?

FRANK. No. Sorry, sergeant, I haven't.

BACON (*writing on the board*). On CBCA. O–N–C–B–C–A. or C–B–A–C–O–N. See Bacon. May I say, from the point of view of a cryptologist, sergeant…

SERGEANT. Cryptologist? No, we're not talking about grave-robbing here, Gandalf. Psychologist! He's changing the way detectives think and work. Groundbreaking.

OXFORD. Is he a Freudian psychologist?

SERGEANT. No, no, no. It's just common sense. Actors! You just don't get us, do you? The man behind the badge. *The Bill, The Sweeney, Dirty Harry,* bunch of ponces. No one can act a copper. Not your true copper. It makes me so angry… You're gonna get this play right, Charlton.

So, pay attention. In a manhunt, like the Ripper case or your Shakespeare question, the success of the detective, I'm talking about a real detective, depends on how well he shapes his mental map and his hunting strategy to match that of his prey, in your case the author, and that's where CBCA comes in. It's a bold chief detective who says, 'MEN...'

He bangs the table as if giving a briefing in an episode of Prime Suspect.

ALL. Yes, sergeant.

SERGEANT. Let's ignore *why* something was done. Instead let's ask what elements can we follow that will lead us to the killer. Close your eyes, men. Because somewhere there, hidden at the scene of the crime, wrapped perhaps in the tiniest of details, with his tiger's heart beating, and his guilty hand still shaking in the darkness, our masked man can't help but reveal his true identity.

The phone rings. They all jump. FRANK *answers as quietly as possible.*

FRANK. Hello. This is Frank Charlton, your host on *Who's There?* The International Authorship Chat Show... play. What's your question?

BARRY. I have a question for Sir Francis Bacon.

FRANK. Yes. Sir Francis, it's for you.

BACON. Hello. This is Francis Bacon.

BARRY. One sugar or two?

BACON. Two please, Barry.

OXFORD. What connection did your colleagues make between the Ripper diary and the authorship controversy?

SERGEANT (*who has been writing on the board*). CBCA. Criteria-Based Content Analysis is an objective test psychologists have fashioned to help determine the authenticity of a written account.

FRANK. Really? Any written account?

SERGEANT. In this case, the diary of James Maybrick, a Victorian cotton merchant, which happens to give a first-person account of the deeds of Jack the Ripper. Is the diary a fabrication drawn from the accounts of others or a description of actual events the author experienced? That's the crucial question.

OXFORD. That is the crucial question.

FRANK. How can you tell if an author has actually experienced something, rather than reported it second hand?

SERGEANT. CBCA says an invention is always more likely to lack the sort of detail a genuine account has – the sort of detail that would be more likely to come from genuine experience than fabrication.

OXFORD. Sergeant, the plays contain descriptions of my travels through Italy in such minute detail that, until recent re-evaluation, they were thought inaccurate. Fourteen plays set in Italy and yet neither of them ever visited Italy.

BACON. They are ill discoverers that think there is no land, when they can see nothing but sea. My brother Anthony travelled extensively in Italy and the Continent before he returned to live and write with me.

SHAKSPAR. Sergeant, what do people do when they return from travels? They talk about what they've experienced. I picked up everything about Italy in the plays from travellers' chat along Bankside.

OXFORD. In the beginning of my play *Romeo and Juliet*, I place Romeo in a sycamore grove, quote: 'that westward rooteth from this city side'. The sycamore trees are still there to the west of Verona today. This is an inconsequential detail drawn from the memory as a writer writes. Why would a traveller chatting about the glories of Renaissance Italy mention some insignificant trees?

SERGEANT. Now you're using your head, copper. Details. I like it.

SHAKSPAR. Surely it's the job of a creative writer to add that sort of convincing detail.

SERGEANT. Now calm down, Shirley Temple. Rambo's right. No writer can help leaving his fingerprints on the scene.

The SERGEANT *gets a call on his radio.*

CBCA finds the irrelevant detail, that little clue that does not really move the storyline forwards and may actually undermine its main purpose.

OXFORD. Tell the sergeant about J. Thomas Looney, Charlton. Show him the evidence.

SERGEANT. Hold on a moment. Charlton, take charge.

He steps out.

OXFORD. The plays are like a self-portrait of my life, Charlton.

SHAKSPAR. Frank. The range of plots and characters in the plays is so vast that you can find 'self-portraits' of anyone you care to think of.

OXFORD. Why is it so hard to find you then? There is only one authentic Warwickshire character, Christopher Sly of *The Taming of the Shrew*; a bearherd who falls down drunk one night outside a nobleman's country manor and wakes to find himself impersonating, God forbid, a nasty aristocrat with a troupe of players... The biographical parallels between my life and the plays are too many to be ignored and too personal to be fabricated. Sixteen months, I toured the Continent: Padua, Mantua, Venice, Sicily. Every familiar Shakespearean setting. I sailed exactly the same route as the boys in *Comedy of Errors* at exactly the same age. I arrived in Italy at the start of a two-month festival of *commedia dell'arte*...

BACON. Was that when you challenged the whole of Palermo to a duel?

OXFORD.... a theatrical form unknown at the time in England and apparent in the Shakespeare comedies.

SHAKSPAR. Frank, you know, I'm not surprised to see he's back from the dead again. The noble Earl of Oxford died in 1604. If he wrote my late plays, he was pushing them up with the daisies!

OXFORD. And the flow of Shakespearean publications died immediately too, didn't it, Will? When I died. A few isolated quartos from certain unidentified 'grand possessors'. But nothing else after my death until the First Folio of 1623.

SHAKSPAR. *The Tempest* was impelled by a sea voyage that took place in 1609; *Macbeth* could not have been composed before the Gunpowder Plot of 1605. It's impossible that you wrote them.

OXFORD. Oh yes, I'm terribly sorry. I forgot that there has only ever been one sea voyage and one treasonous plot in recorded history. Anonymous versions of *Hamlet* and *King Lear* were being performed in the early 1590s. If you wrote these mature plays then you were pushing them out with your first facial hair. Charlton! My family's theatre company was touring to Stratford-upon-Avon when he was still plodding about the provinces performing puppet shows.

[I am praised, during my lifetime, as a comic playwright of excellence, so where are my comedies, if they are not the comedies of Shakespeare? Where are they? My own poetry ceases as soon as the name William Shakespeare appears.

SHAKSPAR. And this man claims to have written 'Brevity is the soul of wit'.]

The SERGEANT *returns with* BARRY *and the drinks.* BARRY *is singing.*

BARRY. I'm a Sputnik Love God.

SERGEANT. Charlton! What the hell's going on here?

FRANK *gets out evidence on boards and flipcharts, while* BARRY *hands round drinks.*

FRANK. We were just talking about the work of J. Thomas Looney. Would you look at this evidence I have, sergeant? In 1920, an English schoolteacher, J. Thomas Looney, employed a new methodology of investigation – very similar to your criteria-based content analysis. He simply examined the Shakespeare plays extremely closely without any preconception of who the author might be; drew from the words what the author knew about and cared about; and determined a list of eighteen attributes of the author's character. Here they are. With this evidence, Looney then set about looking and found a man who had the knowledge and life experience indicated by the writing.

SERGEANT. This is more like it. Good work, Charlton.

FRANK. Plus, I have the literary trail of all the writers of his time – Jonson, Marlowe, Spenser...

SERGEANT. A trail?

FRANK. Yes. The evidence all writers leave; of letters written and received, education, records of being paid for writing, et cetera. As you see, Shakespeare is the only one of twenty-five with no evidence...

SERGEANT....that proves he wrote for a living?

FRANK. During his lifetime. That's right. Not one. Everything is attributed to him after his death. Seven years after his death.

SERGEANT. If writing plays was a crime, it sounds like William Shakespeare would be found innocent.

FRANK. Why, sergeant?

SERGEANT. In a court of law, Charlton, a suspect must be found guilty beyond a reasonable doubt. Any reasonable doubt obliges a jury to judge the accused innocent.

BACON. If a man will begin with certainties, he shall end in doubts; but if he will be content to begin with doubts he shall end in certainties.

OXFORD. From this evidence, sergeant, can you not confirm the character profile of the perpetrator of the Shakespeare plays matches none other than myself, the Earl of Oxford?

SERGEANT. No. This is the most appalling mismanagement of a manhunt I have ever witnessed, Charlton. Slack. If I'm frank, that's what I call this. You're subjecting your men to an overload of information. You've got the whole squad heated up about the rights and wrongs before all the facts have been fully considered.

FRANK. Yes, sergeant.

[SERGEANT. You're wasting valuable police time and putting the theatregoing public at risk. Because you can be damn sure your man is out there somewhere, right now, as we speak, with his words rammed down some poor actor's throat, his thoughts stuffed in some poor audience's head, and no one knows who the hell is doing it!]

FRANK. Yes, sergeant.

SERGEANT. Only acting, Charlton. What did you think? Of my acting?

FRANK. Oh yes. Very good.

SERGEANT. It's a shame you haven't got a Shakespeare diary like Maybrick's Ripper diary.

OXFORD. But there is a diary.

FRANK. There's a Shakespeare diary?

OXFORD. My diary. The Shakespeare sonnets. The author is an older man who knows disgrace, as I did, writing to younger men and women, as here:

> 'That time of year thou mayst in me behold
> When yellow leaves, or none, or few, do hang
> Upon those boughs which shake against the cold,
> Bare ruined choirs where late the sweet birds sang.
> In me thou seest the twilight of such day
> As after sunset fadeth in the west,
> Which by and by black night doth take away,
> Death's second self, that seals up all in rest.
> In me thou seest the glowing of such fire
> That on the ashes of his youth doth lie
> As the deathbed wheron it must expire,
> Consumed with that which it was nourished by.
> This thou perceives, which makes thy love more strong,
> To love that well which thou must leave ere long.'

FRANK. In 1590, when the sonnets begin, you were already forty, while Shakspar and Bacon were still in their twenties.

BACON. Frank. Many of the sonnets are not just personal revelation. Some are hymns of praise for the poet's higher self, his muse, the true genius.

'So oft have I invoked thee for my muse
And found such fair assistance in my verse
As every alien pen hath got my use,
And under thee their poesy disperse.
Thine eyes, that taught the dumb on high to sing
And heavy ignorance aloft to fly,
Have added feathers to the learned's wing
And given grace a double majesty.
Yet be most proud of that which I compile,
Whose influence is thine and born of thee.
In others' works thou dost but mend the style,
And arts with thy sweet graces graced be;
But thou art all my art, and dost advance
As high as learning my rude ignorance.'

FRANK. The Advancement of Learning! Your great work.

SHAKSPAR.

'If thy soul check thee that I come so near,
Swear to thy blind soul that I was thy Will,
And will, thy soul knows, is admitted there;
Thus far for love my love-suit, sweet, fulfil.
Will will fulfil the treasure of thy love,
Ay, fill it full with wills, and my will one.
In things of great receipt with ease we prove
Among a number one is reckoned none.
Then in the number let me pass untold,
Though in thy store's account I one must be;
For nothing hold me, so it please thee hold
That nothing me a something, sweet, to thee.
Make but my name thy love, and love that still,
And then thou lov'st me for my name is Will.'

Not Edward! Not Francis! Will! My name is Will.

He storms out and down the driveway. BARRY *in pursuit.*

OXFORD. Will means a sense of resolve, a sexual passion.
Would Sir Philip Sidney write a poem, 'my name is Phil'?

SHAKSPAR. It's a pun. It's got more than one meaning.
Wordplay. That's what I do.

SERGEANT. Come back here.

BARRY. Wait, Will, mate! Will!

SERGEANT. Actors! You've got a mutiny on your hands, Charlton. Well, Shakespeare or not, I now have to take this clown down to the station for resisting arrest.

The SERGEANT *starts to take* OXFORD *out of the garage.*

Scene Two

The Fourth Guest Ever: Mary Sidney Herbert

MARY SIDNEY HERBERT, *the* COUNTESS OF PEMBROKE, *to whose sons the First Folio was dedicated, appears at the back door.* FRANK, *the* SERGEANT, BACON *and* OXFORD *are in the garage.* BARRY *and* SHAKSPAR *have gone.*

MARY. Frank, darling, I have never been more ashamed in my life. You're absolutely right to look at me that way. I'm not just late; I've missed the entire rehearsal. The golden rule, the one thing that separates professional actors from amateurs, is timing. I've let you all down. You've probably written me out of the scene. And I deserve it…

FRANK. I don't know what…

SERGEANT. Excuse me…

MARY. It's no excuse, but Harold took the wrong turn and then there was an accident, it was nothing, but these two young men, the drivers, were so 'het up'; 'road rage', you know, really you'd think young men today were connected to their automobiles by an umbilical cord. Anyway, Harold, my chauffeur, he's so conscientious, used to be a policeman, about your height, and… well, my dears, only when… I'm so sorry, we haven't met, are you playing the policeman?

SERGEANT. No, madam, I am a policeman.

MARY. Oh my Lord, has there been an accident?

SERGEANT. No, madam.

MARY. What on earth has Edward done now? He didn't knock
your cap off, did he?

SERGEANT. Yes, as a matter of fact he did.

MARY. Oh my Lord! He thought you were Harold dressed up
as the policeman.

SERGEANT. Harold?

MARY. Harold, my chauffeur. He was going to play the
policeman today.

SERGEANT. Your chauffeur was going to pretend to be a
policeman here today?

MARY. Yes, that's right. As part of our play.

SERGEANT. That's what Charlton said but I still don't believe
Mr de Vere was acting.

MARY. He's terribly good, isn't he? Was he about to kill
William Shakespeare when you arrived?

SERGEANT. Yes.

MARY. Oh, I love that bit. And then did William shout, 'Help
me, master constable, this man intends to murder me!' and
when you took hold of Lord Oxford, did he say, 'Unhand
me, constable, by Heaven, I'll make a ghost of him that lets
me.' And then knock your helmet off your head and call you
a dog. Is that how it happened?

SERGEANT. Yes, yes, yes, that's exactly how it took place.
How did you know that?

MARY. It's in the script.

SERGEANT. But why didn't Mr de Vere stop when he realised
I was a policeman?

MARY. Because Edward's one of Stanleywalskie's method
actors, and he thought you were Harold, my ex-constable
chauffeur, exploring an emotional-recall exercise. It's very
bad form not to play along. Isn't that right, Edward?

OXFORD. Whatever.

MARY. If you left him with us, Harold could bring him straight over to the police station after rehearsal and help you torture him.

OXFORD. What?

SERGEANT. I beg your pardon?

MARY. Why, what did you do?

BACON. I think you meant 'question him', Lady Mary.

MARY. Did I? I'm so sorry.

SERGEANT. Your driver used to be a policeman? Who are you?

MARY. I apologise. You can call me Lady Mary. You've had such a shock. Sit down a moment.

She gets the SERGEANT *to sit down. He is quite taken with her.*

Harold's more than enough to restrain Edward if he loses it again. Once a policeman, always a policeman. You can tell by the look in the eyes.

SERGEANT. Can you?

MARY. Of course you can. Always looking ahead. Always prepared for the unexpected. Always helping people.

SERGEANT. And you say he'll be right back?

MARY. Yes, sergeant.

SERGEANT. Do you have an important part in the play, Lady Mary?

MARY. It depends on Mr Charlton.

SERGEANT. Look. Here's my telephone number. Ring me if you have any trouble. Charlton, I might come and see your play. You better get it right.

He releases OXFORD.

I hold you responsible for Mr de Vere's appearance at the station tonight.

FRANK. Thank you, sergeant.

SERGEANT. It's been a pleasure to meet you, Mary.

MARY. The pleasure's entirely mine.

SERGEANT. Always looking ahead. I like that. Very observant of you. Think smart, men.

He goes.

MARY. Now, Santa, where's Shirley Temple?

They celebrate.

BACON. Mr Charlton, may I introduce my cousin, Lady Mary Sidney.

FRANK. Mary Sidney.

OXFORD. The Countess of Pembroke

FRANK. What are you doing here?

MARY. Mr Charlton. The First Folio of Shakespeare's plays was dedicated to my sons, the incomparable brethren. I think I can shed some light on this question of the authorship. You don't have any tobacco, do you? Cigarettes?

FRANK. You smoke?

MARY. Yes, I did a lot of things that were forbidden to women in my day. Took it up in France when I was abroad with my forbidden lover, Dr Lister.

FRANK. Who forbids a countess?

MARY. My son, William Herbert, in this instance, Mr W.H. Beneath-My-Class, you know, forbidden relations across class boundaries, like so many of the love affairs in the Shakespeare works. Aren't they wonderful characters, Mr Charlton, the women, I mean? Such independence, in a society where women were still considered property. Some even thought us without a soul. Can you imagine! It still delights me to see so many who defy male domination in the plays. A distinguishing feature of the Shakespeare plays, wouldn't you agree?

FRANK. Yes, I suppose so, I'd never thought of that before...

MARY. Oh yes, do you know, at least sixteen marry the man of their choice. Nine even defying their fathers to do so. Thank God, things have got – a little bit – better since then.

FRANK. Would you mind if I filmed you?

MARY. Of course not, that's what I'm here for.

OXFORD. Charlton. There are numerous fringe claims like this. They just distract from the truth and play into the hands of Stratfordians.

MARY. My lord, if you will hear me out. How could a...

OXFORD. How could a man conceive a character like Rosalind or Cleopatra? How could a woman conceive the men?

MARY. You mean the murderers, overbearing fathers, insanely jealous husbands, pompous pedants, drunkards, cowards, liars, extortionists, hypocrites, and dimwits? I don't know. Direct life experience? Don't you find it curious, Mr Charlton, why so much fuss is made about what Shakespeare thought of women? They are far and away the better represented gender – intelligent, capable women – women I find it hard to imagine emerging from your imagination, my lord.

OXFORD. Some of them took quite a bit of imagination.

MARY. Have you read my translation of the play, *The Tragedie of Anthony*, Mr Charlton?

FRANK. No, I'm afraid I haven't. But I think I've got it here.

OXFORD. Closet drama.

BACON. Mary was the first woman in England to publish a play, Frank.

OXFORD. A translation of a play.

MARY. Women were only allowed to publish translations, or eulogies for the dead, and even then with wretched apologies for even assuming to write. The anguish of enforced anonymity you bemoan, cousin, really. Get a life. Is that the expression?

FRANK. Yes, that's it.

MARY. Get a life! I do adore this modern English. Only Elizabeth could write without apology, but then she did everything without apology, didn't she, boys? If you need a cause, a reason, for writing anonymously behind an obvious pseudonym like Shakespeare, try being a woman in my time.

FRANK. Are you saying a woman wrote Shakespeare?

MARY. Perhaps things haven't changed after all.

FRANK. I mean, your *Antony and Cleopatra* is obviously a major inspiration for the Shakespeare play, but translated historical drama is just an academic exercise...

MARY. Quite the contrary, I used the idea of translated historical drama as a veiling device to tell the truth.

BACON. Give a man a mask and he'll tell you the truth.

MARY.
     'Invest in me, my motley. Give me leave
     To speak my mind...'

OXFORD.
              '...and I will through and through
     Cleanse the foul body of th'infected world...'

MARY. You see, we were all brought up as children on visiting players, and plays, adapted by our relatives to express some hidden message, joke or reformation propaganda. What do you think the play scene in *Hamlet* is based on, pure fantasy?

BACON.
              'I have heard
     That guilty creatures sitting at a play...'

MARY.
     'Have by the very cunning of the scene...'

BACON.
     'Been struck so to the soul that presently...'

MARY.
     'They have proclaimed their malefactions...'

OXFORD.
>   'I'll have these players
>   Play something like the murder of my father
>   Before mine uncle. I'll observe his looks…
>
>   The play's the thing
>   Wherein I'll catch the conscience of the King.'

FRANK. But your private drama is a world apart from the commercial playhouses of Bankside.

MARY. Only in scale. As play-making was for us in our ruling families, so it was for the people: the first functional step towards freedom of speech behind the mask of harmless entertainment.

BACON. The voice of the people.

OXFORD. The birth of the commercial theatre and press was as radical a revolution in our age as the birth of the internet is in yours. No one could control it.

BACON. For the first time in England's history, the production of plays and books was not dependent on wealthy patrons.

OXFORD. You see, Charlton, no one else in Europe spoke or wrote or read English. It was rare to hear it even in Wales, Ireland or Scotland. Most people had an extremely low opinion of our own language, so some of us began to write; to create a body of literature in the English language which would match the Greek and Latin classics we so admired.

MARY. Our English Literary Renaissance…

FRANK. Our?

MARY. Mr Charlton, your search for a literary superhero of mind, heart and body, makes for compelling drama. We played out such fantasies in our age as well. The Virgin Queen being the most renowned.

BACON. Cousin.

MARY. Why? She can't touch us now.

OXFORD. Speak what we feel, not what we ought to say.

MARY. With respect, I will speak as I wish, gentlemen. Mr Charlton, has any revolution ever been created by one man or woman alone? Revolutionary movements may gather around an inspiring leader or two, but sustained revolutions require a group to accomplish any set of common goals in a way that lasts.

FRANK. Are you suggesting…

MARY. Great art is not created in a vacuum.

FRANK. Who comprised this revolutionary literary group?

MARY (*laughs*). Which one? Raleigh's school of night? Francis's good pens at Twickenham? My lord's euphuistic school in Shoreditch? Montaigne and Ronsard's French circle in Paris, the Pleiades? Or my Areopagus of English writers, the Wilton Circle, on the banks of the Avon?

FRANK. You had a school of writers in Stratford-upon-Avon?

MARY. There are several river Avon in England, Mr Charlton, the one in Wiltshire ran through my property at Wilton House, where I gathered the greatest writers of English I could find to fulfil my brother's vision.

BACON. 'The beloved sweet swan of Avon.'

MARY. Yes, my brother, Philip, and I were often referred to as swans, because our French friends enjoyed the connection between Sidney and Cygny. *Le Cygne*. Many poets referred to me as such.

FRANK. Did you write the works of Shakespeare!

MARY. Let me paint an alternative scenario for you. One that is not quite so anachronistic to our time as your modern concept of lone heroic authors in garrets, *Shakespeare in Love*, and all that schoolgirl romance.

As she speaks, MARY *takes down books by the authors she is naming from* FRANK'*s shelves and places them in a pile on the floor.*

If you look at the records, there exist a number of Elizabethan writers from modest backgrounds who lack anything resembling a writer's biography. Their purported works, replete with courtly themes and expression, do not match what the records suggest about their life experiences. They are: Richard Edwards, Edmund Spenser, George Pettie, John Lyly, Robert Greene, Thomas Watson, Thomas Nashe, John Webster, and…

FRANK. William Shakespeare.

MARY. Correct. These writers are matched by a second group of courtly writers, who have little or nothing published under their own names and yet are reported to have written extensively or with particular poetic quality.

FRANK. Or, if they do publish extensively, like Sir Francis, their extant works do not provide the kind of writing which they are reported to have done.

MARY. Correct. They are: the Earl of Oxford, Francis Bacon, Sir Walter Raleigh, the Earl of Derby…

FRANK. And yourself.

MARY.…and myself.

FRANK (*referring to the books on the floor*). So, we have plays in the names of these men but little or no evidence that they were playwrights, while you five, reported to be brilliant poets and playwrights, leave us no plays.

MARY. Not only these five. This second group includes two more, whose works of poetry and drama are attributed to them, but only after their untimely deaths. The sixth author was the kind of man that Stratfordians wish William Shakspar was, a true natural genius, the brilliant shoemaker's son from Canterbury, my dear Christopher Marlowe.

BACON. His terrible departure was part of the inspiration to dedicate our works to a common man. We were honouring his genius.

FRANK. You knew Christopher Marlowe?

MARY. Yes. Very well. Christopher's assassination or exile made our secrecy a necessity.

FRANK. He was exiled?

MARY. Walsingham would never have had him killed. But murdered or exiled – either way, silence... we knew...

OXFORD. The game was up. Have you never wondered why the Shakespeare name is first used a few weeks after Marlowe's disappearance? If Mr Shakspar wrote the plays, why publish under his own name for the first time then, when it was so dangerous?

FRANK. Who was the seventh author in this literary group?

BACON. Her brilliant brother, Sir Philip Sidney. And my beloved brother, Anthony.

MARY. Yes, your brilliant brother, though even more hidden.

OXFORD. Marlowe and Sydney could only be published under their own names because they had been killed.

FRANK. You're saying these men were the stand-ins whose names were employed to protect the identity of the real writers?

OXFORD. Why would the author of the Shakespeare plays be the only one who had to hide? In the new world, during that Senator McCarthy's witch-hunts, was Dalton Trumbo the only Hollywood screenwriter forced to use a front?

FRANK. Who?

OXFORD. Dalton Trumbo, the man who wrote *Spartacus*.

FRANK. That's who wrote *Spartacus*! Who in this group did what? I mean, who wrote the works of Shakespeare?

MARY. We all contributed in a number of ways. We influenced each other. Supported each other. Criticised each other. But always in secret.

FRANK. Surely one of you was the prime author of the works of Shakespeare.

BACON. They say that Love was the most ancient of all the gods, without parent, the prime author of all things whatever, except Chaos, divine Chaos, out of which Love begot all things, there being nothing before it. It is the cause.

FRANK. Did you write together?

MARY. If you take note of the literary approach in writing: the habits of expression, and the unchanging personal concerns that transcend all efforts to alter style and genre; pay close attention to dates; and consider the reflection of events and issues of the authors' personal lives, you will discover the truth. Nothing truer than the truth.

There is a power cut and the lights go out.

FRANK. Don't panic. It's just a power cut.

FRANK fetches a torch and lights candles. Stars are visible in the sky above the garage – a moon too, Diana.

Beautiful and mysterious music arises during the scene. The actors become increasingly still as the subject reaches its most personal manifestation.

MARY. What a relief. Really, how do you bear all this light everywhere?

FRANK. But what did *you* write?

MARY. Have you ever compared *The Duchess of Malfi* or *The White Devil* with my work?

FRANK. John Webster. Of course. John Webster's life shows even less connection to any literary or theatrical activity than Shakspar's. Those two masterpieces have remarkably strong women in the lead roles, like the Shakespeare plays and depend primarily, for their source, on the Countess of Pembroke's *Arcadia*.

MARY. Which I and my lover wrote together.

BACON. Look. One can finally see the stars again. See Cassiopeia. The double-A in the constellation of the virgin. Did you know there was a supernova right in the middle of Cassiopeia in 1572, Frank? We all took it to be the sign of a virgin birth of the arts and poetry under our virgin queen Elizabeth.

FRANK. Wait a minute. I thought the Countess of Pembroke's *Arcadia* was your completed version of Sir Philip Sidney's work?

MARY. It was.

FRANK. But you just said that you wrote it with your lover.

MARY. The father of my two sons, the incomparable brethren of the First Folio.

FRANK. You wrote it with William Herbert, their father?

MARY. I wrote it with my lover, Philip Sidney.

FRANK. You had an incestuous relationship with your brother Philip Sidney?

MARY. No, I did not. Though I could never deny it in my life. He wasn't my brother, because I wasn't a Sidney. I was the daughter of someone else, someone who sent him to die on the battlefields of the Netherlands, fighting for her kingdom because of what he did.

BACON. Mary.

MARY.
> 'For his honour, it stuck upon him as the sun
> In the grey vault of heaven, and by his light
> Did all the chivalry of England move
> To do brave acts. He was indeed the glass
> Wherein the noble youth did dress themselves.
> In speech, in gait, in diet, in affections of delight,
> In military rules, humours of blood,
> He was the mark and glass, copy and book,
> That fashioned others. And him – O wondrous him!
> O miracle of men – him did she leave,
> Second to none, unseconded by her,
> To look upon the hideous god of war
> In disadvantage…'

You see, I sometimes write of men. I wasn't allowed to attend his funeral. I was twenty-five years old. He had been my life.

BACON *comforts* MARY SIDNEY.

BACON. She lost her father and her brother in twelve months. You fell so ill you very nearly died yourself. She mourned for two years, Frank.

FRANK. The Countess Olivia in *Twelfth Night*… also loses both her father and brother within a year.

BACON. Yes, Frank. But Philip's death only fired your determination to continue what you both had started, didn't it, cousin?

OXFORD. It's true, the Sidneys were to the English Renaissance what the Medici were to the Florentine.

FRANK. So you were a part of this secret literary renaissance, Lord Oxford?

OXFORD. I had my own group. Philip and I quarrelled.

BACON. An unfortunate encounter on a tennis court.

OXFORD. We made it up later, as families do.

FRANK. Families?

BACON. My Lord Oxford.

OXFORD. I am I, however I was begot. How elaborately guarded you taught us all to be, my careful little cousin. How well you hid your humiliation…

BACON. My lord.

OXFORD. Hid from yourself… constructing histories and tables of anger, fear, ambition; reasoned essays on emotion. Hiding from your true nature behind theories of man's dominance over nature through art and science.

BACON. I have never in my life advocated man's dominance over nature. Quite the contrary, my humble proposal is that we must serve nature if we are to master nature, our own nature as well as the nature of the universe. The Shakespeare works deserve a much wider canvas than the one provided for a self-portrait, no matter how true to nature that may be.

OXFORD. It's time that people understood the cause of Shakespeare, Charlton. This empty Stratford biography is breeding an art empty of humanity, empty of nature itself. Unless an artist puts himself into his creation, puts the very chaotic centre of his being into the work, there's no point, nothing. A true biographical approach will liberate the work from all this nullifying modern scholarship. Up its ass in intellectual theory with no relevance to life, no blood, no soul, no royal note...

BACON. Edward.

OXFORD. The note of royalty, the unavoidable unique note of Shakespeare. The question of what constitutes true kingship is not so much a theme in Shakespeare, as an obsession. And the crown he seeks time and again, is not the gilded crown of power and money, but the simple band of truth.

MARY. And what is that truth, my lord, that you must speak so loudly?

BACON. Ah, what is truth said...

OXFORD. That Shakespeare's a bastard for all ages. An eternal exile searching for his kingdom in the imagined worlds of theatre. He was compelled to write. He is the monstrous adversary, the strange majestic chaos at the heart of our lives, the sweet, sweet, poison for the age's tooth, in everything illegitimate...

FRANK. Illegitimate? Are you all illegitimate children?

OXFORD. Each of us, in our own way, trying to legitimise our time, our true nature, in words. Words in the mouths of vagabonds dressed as kings.

Pause.

Very still.

FRANK. Bastardy. The royal note of Shakespeare. Exile, disinheritance, one's origin concealed – an island, a dark forest, a cave... bastards.

BACON. Only those things that are light and puffed-up float in the river of time. Those which are weighty and solid, sink.

OXFORD. The dark secrets of Fortuna. Being the child of a virgin means you don't exist.

MARY. Other than in the imagination.

OXFORD. Where do people exist who don't exist?

FRANK. In the theatre.

Scene Three

Barry and Shakspar Return for the Truth

We hear rocks and clods of earth hitting the galvanised-steel roof of the garage.

We hear BARRY *and* SHAKSPAR *enter up the driveway in a drunken fashion carrying things to throw.*

BARRY *and* SHAKSPAR. Howl, howl, howl, howl!

BARRY. O you are men of stones.

SHAKSPAR. You do me wrong to take me out of the grave. Dost thou think because thou art virtuous there shall be no more cakes and ale?

BARRY. It was quiz night at The Coach and Horses, Frank. No education! Look at this, Frank.

BARRY *points out the large, yellow, first-prize badge* SHAKSPAR *wears.*

First prize! First prize in the pub quiz! The man's a genius. They've all come round.

BARRY *speaks with the audience as if they are people from the local pub surrounding the garage. Real names of people in the audience each night would be good.*

Here we are, everyone. Hello, [Mrs Dysart]. This is his garage. Hello, [Mr Jones]. Just like I told you. They're all in there. We're all here, Frank. All your neighbours. Come up from the pub. Why? Because we love the man. We love Shakespeare.

O Shakespeare, wilt thou come no more?

BARRY *and* SHAKSPAR. Never, never, never, never, never. You'll never walk alone!

FRANK. Barry, come in here. The Countess of Pembroke is here.

BARRY. Don't tell me a countess wrote the plays. How many more Shakespeares are we expecting, Frank?

SHAKSPAR. Oh, there are hundreds and that's not counting all the committees. What did a committee ever create?

BARRY. Yeah, everybody! A starter for ten. What's a group of people ever made that hasn't been total crap? *The Life of Brian*. 'Hey Jude.' *Friends. The Simpsons*. The Bible. But apart from that!

SHAKSPAR. You'll end up insane, Frank. How much more of this madness can you take? Come out of there! It's the plays that matter. They're just good entertainment. I'm just an ordinary man like you with a big imagination. Just enjoy the plays. What does it matter who wrote them?

The lights come back on inside the garage.

OXFORD. It's time you made up your mind, Charlton. At least kick one of us out. Narrow the field. Surely it's time you sent Shakspar packing.

BARRY. Send Shakspar packing! Friends, Romans, people from the pub, put down your beers!

Look at him. Look at my friend Will. He's waited three hundred and ninety-something fuckin' years to return to England, the least he could have expected was 'Well done, mate' – 'I don't understand a fucking word of what you wrote, I had a crap teacher, I hated Shakespeare in school, you wouldn't catch me dead at a play of yours, but, you know, well done.' 'You did it.' 'You're a classic.' What's he get instead? 'Fuck off, you impostor, fake, poser, fucking Midlands idiot!' You come to bury Shakespeare, Frank, not to praise him!

What about all the poor people of Stratford-upon-Avon? What's Stratford got if it doesn't have Shakespeare? The butterfly house. If you prove Shakespeare didn't write the plays, Frank, there will be refugees for miles around, unemployed, shocked Stratfordians clogging up the roads to Birmingham. And, it will be your fault. Why don't you come out and ask your neighbours who wrote Shakespeare? I bet they know. Let's sort this whole thing out once and for all.

OXFORD. I want to speak with the neighbours. I would like to answer their questions directly.

MARY. It would certainly be refreshing to hear the opinions of some other women.

BACON. Ah, that the increase of natural light and the way of the senses had not thrown the divine mysteries into darkness and incredulity. I fear, my lord, that every man still takes the limit of his vision to be the limit of the world – but let us hear the voice of the people.

OXFORD *opens the garage doors at the front of the garage and turns on an outdoor light.* BARRY *nips in and picks up a microphone he has attached to his sound system. He emcee's the conversation through his sound system as the actors move amongst the audience as if they were people from the pub sitting in* FRANK's *garden. They ask them what they think, and pass some comments back to* BARRY *and* FRANK. *The company improvises. Sometimes, in performance, against* FRANK's *better judgement,* BARRY *insisted on a vote. These votes usually elected* SHAKSPAR *as the author.* FRANK's *refusal to accept this result provoked the next scene. But I leave this improvised section to the artistry of the company.*

Scene Four

Shakspar and the Angry Boar

The SERGEANT'S TWIN BROTHER *enters from the back of the auditorium, if possible he has slipped into a seat. He is dressed in civilian clothes. Sometimes foam comes from his mouth like the boar in* Venus and Adonis. *He is furious.*

TWIN. I'm sorry. I've had enough. I've had it. I've had enough of this rubbish. I can't take it any more!

FRANK. Sergeant?

TWIN. I'm not a sergeant. That's my brother. You call yourself
a teacher. What are you teaching our boys and girls?

FRANK. I'm teaching them to question, to think for
themselves.

TWIN. If you can question who Shakespeare is, you can
question anything. Anything! Some things just *are*! And
Shakespeare's one of them! I blame the internet. Is nothing
sacred any more! And as for you, I don't know who you
think you are, dressing up as Shakespeare for Charlton's
internet propaganda, but you ought to be ashamed.
ASHAMED of yourself. What do you think Shakespeare
would think of you? You're a traitor to your own profession.
All of you, traitors! Biting the hand that feeds you. BITING!
BITING! BITING!

SHAKSPAR. Actually, you've got the wrong end of the spear,
sir. It's you who's the problem.

TWIN. How dare you speak to me like that?

SHAKSPAR. I've spent the last couple of hours with this man.
I've fought with him. I've shouted at him like you are, but all
he's doing is asking a question. A natural question that arises
from the way I lived my life, and God knows I wish I had
kept better records.

TWIN. This is what has become of our modern-day actors.
Instead of acting Shakespeare for the RSC, they're paid to
dress up like a Shakespeare-a-like and insult our intelligence.
This is what happens if you listen to heretics!

SHAKSPAR. My plays are not a religion. Questions and doubt
have always been a part of my work. My God, if theatre
people hadn't doubted how my plays were actually
performed, we'd still have happy songs at the end of *King
Lear*! We'd still have jolly dances in *Macbeth*. My plays are
all about questioning, challenging, confronting our sense of
identity! That's all he's doing!

The TWIN *pushes* SHAKSPAR *and* SHAKSPAR *knocks
him out.*

Scene Five

The Link is Broken

Everyone retreats back into the garage, carrying the TWIN, *who is gradually recovering enough to stagger with them.*

FRANK. Close the door, someone!

MARY. He needs some ice. Take him through to the house.

The authors lead the TWIN *out of the back door towards the house, as* FRANK *speaks with the audience/neighbours. He tries but can't close the garage door. It remains a public scene.*

FRANK. Goodnight, everybody. We'll take him to the hospital. Safe home.

TWIN. I'm going to have you for assault, Charlton.

FRANK. All under control now.

TWIN. I'm going to report you to my brother.

FRANK. Look what you've done, Barry! He's punched the policeman's brother.

BARRY. Frank, the cops will be here any minute.

FRANK. I know. I know. Let me think.

BARRY. What are you gonna tell them, Frank? Who did it? A cyberspace Shakespeare?

FRANK. Look, shut up, Barry. Shut the hell up.

BARRY. You've got no idea. A policeman's twin brother has been punched in the face, and I'm going to be implicated.

FRANK. What, you think they're going to throw you into prison? It's my bloody garage.

BARRY. Yeah! Because I'm a celebrity. If a celebrity is involved, they always make an example of him.

FRANK. No one even knows who you are, Barry.

BARRY. That copper knew who I was!

FRANK. He did not.

BARRY. He did. He lingered over my name.

FRANK (*losing it*). Get over it! Get a life! You were famous once for about three months, but no one cares any more. No one! You haven't written a decent song in twenty-two years.

BARRY. You said you loved that chord progression I wrote last April. You said it reminded you of David Bowie when he was a spider from Mars.

FRANK. No, Barry. You said that and I agreed with you.

BARRY. Yeah, you agreed.

FRANK. I lied. Barry. I lied.

BARRY. You lied?

FRANK. You were a novelty act, that's all, a novelty act, not a pop star. I'm fed up pretending.

BARRY. After all I've done for you. The hours I have wasted trying to help you with your stupid authorship obsession. The most pointless subject in the world.

The authors return.

FRANK. Pointless? You said, this afternoon, you said the authorship question had changed your life for ever.

BARRY. Yeah, well, maybe I lied too. Donna was right about you.

MARY. Who's Donna?

BARRY. Donna was Frank's wife until she divorced him a couple of months ago.

FRANK. Barry!

BARRY. Left him a year ago.

FRANK. Barry!

BARRY. Took the kids and went home to her mother.
(*Including the audience/people in the pub.*) Didn't she,
everyone?

FRANK. I told you never to mention her, Barry.

BARRY. I loved your Donna, and little Hermione and
Benedick. The hours I spent trying to comfort her, convince
her to stay with Frank. I admired her.

FRANK. Well, she thought you were an idiot.

BARRY. She never.

FRANK. She hated your music.

BARRY. She never. I wrote 'Donna in My Eyes, a Diamond'
especially for her. She loved it. She cried when she first
heard it.

FRANK. She chucked it in the bin, soon as she came home,
laughing.

BARRY. You're sick, mate. You're sick and you're cruel and
you're greedy.

FRANK. Greedy. Greedy, Barry. What a devastating use of the
English language you have, Barry.

BARRY. You are greedy, you prick. This whole authorship thing
is greedy. You're not satisfied with what you've got. You
want more.

FRANK. It's about the truth, Barry. It's about facing up to the
truth about who we are and where we came from...

BARRY. He's the ultimate creepy fan, trying to get closer to his
beloved fantasy lover Shakespeare, one of you, trying to get
some intimate new shot, some new angle... who's there?
Wanker Franker. Shakespeare's greatest friend. The man who
saved Shakespeare.

FRANK. Listen, Barry: if you don't shut up about my personal
life, I'm going to wipe all of your songs, all your precious
babies, from the face of reality for ever.

BARRY *tries to move in on* FRANK. FRANK *picks up the
Korg keyboard like it is a big gun.*

BARRY. Don't you touch my babies.

FRANK has his finger on a button on the Korg.

FRANK. You come one step nearer or say another word about my personal life and that's it.

BARRY. That's my legacy. My pension.

FRANK. I'm going to wipe 'em all to hell, Barry.

BARRY grabs the power cord of the computer router high on a shelf opposite FRANK.

BARRY. You kill my babies and I'll send your astral pals packing back to their astral plane! And then you'll never know.

FRANK. Take your hand away from that computer router.

BACON. Don't do it, Barry.

OXFORD. We haven't finished what we came to do.

MARY. I only just got here.

Pause.

SHAKSPAR. Pull it, Barry!

In this Tarantino-like moment of suspense, BARRY is so surprised by SHAKSPAR's vehemence that he pulls the plug on the computer and FRANK pushes the delete button. There is an explosion. Smoke. The candidates disappear in a beautiful backward jig.

When they are gone, emptiness, ruin.

BARRY picks up his Korg and goes to the back door.

BARRY. I only came round for some guttering. Who's here? Frank! When the neighbours came round tonight, how many of them did you know? How many did you know by name? You're so busy trying to figure out Shakespeare's name, I'm surprised you remember my name. Who's here, Frank? Knock, knock, who's here? I'm packing it in, Frank. I'm going to go home for a while, think things over. Go out to the Isle of Man, see my old dad. See you when it rains.

He goes. FRANK goes to the door.

Scene Six

Frank's Iambic Nervous Breakdown

Left on his own in the ruin of his garage.

FRANK (*partly to the audience, as if neighbours are still lingering or drifting away, and partly to himself*). Did you see that? They just disappeared. I can explain.

A sudden realisation.

I filmed it. It doesn't matter. I filmed it. I recorded it. I've got it all. The whole thing's in the camera.

FRANK *goes to the camera and begins to rewind the tape.*

I've got the undiscovered personal Shakespeare letter, the missing manuscript, the lost play, *Love's Labour's Won*. Better than that. I've got the most important Shakespeare discovery in three hundred and ninety years! This will show them... up at the Shakespeare Institute!

As he fantasises, FRANK *attaches the camera to the television, and moves it to the front of the garage for the neighbours to see.*

Ah, Professor Greenblatt, Professor Wells, Professor Bate, come in, come in, how good of you to drop by. Yes, this is where it happened. This is where we all sat and talked together. Sorry, what? You've been waiting for three-and-a-half hours. I'm sorry. I've been so busy answering emails and speaking with the media about my upcoming book and lecture tour and... Ring-a-ring-a-ring.

Pretends the phone rings.

Oh, there it goes again... would you excuse me a moment? Hello, who is it, Donna? Michael Wood, the BBC historian? I'm sorry, I can't speak to Mike right now. Excuse me, professors.

FRANK *begins to play the camera but only snow appears on the television screen. He forwards it.*

What, Professor Bate? Did William Shakspar mention your book about him? No, none of the authors mentioned any of your work. Now, come on, professors, you know I just can't understand a word you're saying when you all cry like that. Have some tissues.

Again, snow. Again he forwards it.

Oh, that's very sweet of you to give me an honorary degree, but you know I haven't got room on my little garage wall because of this framed letter rejecting my PhD on the reasonable doubt of Shakespeare's authorship case.

Again, snow.

Where is it? Where is it? It hasn't recorded it. It hasn't recorded anything. Snow. Nothing but snow. Nothing. Nothing will come of nothing.

We hear old recordings of Shakespeare spoken by a range of famous old actors. The tracks repeat and echo in a mysterious way, almost as if in conversation with FRANK.

HAMLET 1. How all occasions do inform against me!

HAMLET 2. Who's there? Nay answer me. Stand and unfold yourself!

FRANK (*unnerved at first as if someone is just outside the back or front door*). Who's there? Who's here? Who's here? Who's there? Nobody?

HAMLET 1 (*repeated, broken, increasing in volume in the background*). Now I am alone.

FRANK. There's nothing there. There's no one here.

Oh, let me not be mad. Not mad. Oh, let me not be mad.

Voices are heard with each line spoken by a different voice. All taken from live performances in full play. The first line of Lear's should repeat under it all.

VOICES. Oh, let me not be mad. Not mad. Oh, let me not be mad.

It's Greek to me.

It's not fair play.

They vanished in thin air.

I'm tongue-tied.

Hoodwinked.

I haven't slept a wink.

The game is up.

For goodness' sake.

Just send me packing.

But me no buts.

A laughing stock.

A bloody-minded…

…blinking idiot.

The truth will out.

Why, be that as it may…

FRANK. The more I try to think about myself – the more I think in Shakespeare's words.

VOICES. My thoughts be bloody or be nothing worth.

FRANK. If I can't imagine or express myself without being influenced by the imagination and words of William Shakespeare…

VOICES. Life's but a walking shadow.

FRANK. And I don't know who William Shakespeare is…

VOICES. Who's there! Nay answer me. Stand and unfold yourself!

The voices of scholars are heard. A separate expert's voice for each profession. Speeding up and overlapping.

William Shakespeare must have been an expert soldier, sailor...

Doctor...

Lawyer...

Money-grubbing...

Traveller...

Gardener...

Statesman...

Sportsman...

Catholic...

Pagan...

Protestant...

Hermeticist...

Alchemist...

Man o'the people...

Man of the court...

That struts and frets...

FRANK. Who am I? Which one am I? Who am I?

VOICES. Oh, Romeo, Romeo, wherefore art thou, Romeo?

FRANK. I can't seem to think... to speak...

The voices build to a crescendo.

VOICES. Speak the speech, I pray you! As I pronounced it to you.

FRANK. Shut up. For God's sake, will you shut up, Shakespeare!

VOICES. How long has thou been a grave maker?

FRANK. No!

VOICES. That is the question...

FRANK. Why?

VOICES. Is it not monstrous that this player here?

FRANK. Let me be! Let me be! Let be.

> FRANK *takes a bust of Shakespeare and smashes it on the ground.*

Scene Seven

The Tree Sonnet

FRANK *hears the voices of the four authors as they gently speak this sonnet to him.*

MARY. What child draws roots when sketching their first tree?

FRANCIS. The trunk, the branches, leaves and ground will do.

MARY. At some point someone tells the child to see…

FRANCIS. That what's above exists below it too.

MARY. And what's below is spread as wide above…

FRANCIS. See B, see A, see A, see B, the same.

WILLIAM. Who owns that oak that all the neighbours love?

EDWARD. The one whose fence surrounds it in his name?

WILLIAM. The oak's boughs shade the whole community…

EDWARD. Who garden where the hidden roots are sunk…

WILLIAM. The spreading, deepening, biographies…

EDWARD. Invisibly sustaining boughs and trunk?

FRANCIS. Who owns a tree, Frank…

MARY. when the creeping vine…

EDWARD. Idolatry…

WILLIAM. …begins to name it mine?

Scene Eight

Frank Finds Kirk Douglas on His Drive

FRANK. Who owns the oak that all the neighbours love?

What's in a name? Suppose we all agreed upon the name, we'd still imagine many different Shakespeares. What's in a name?

FRANK's *recording of the film* Spartacus *comes onto the screen of the television. The image perhaps also appears above on the heavenly screens so that all can see it.*

Oh, this is my favourite scene. Have you seen this?

It's the scene where Olivier is hunting for Spartacus after the failed uprising. We see Olivier looking from his horse. We see Kirk begin to stand up and then Tony stands up for him and says he himself is Spartacus. Then we see other slaves stand up and claim to be Spartacus in order to hide and protect him.

When the slaves stand up to shout 'I am Spartacus!', FRANK *stands up too.*

I am Spartacus! You'll never find him, Sir Laurence! He's hidden himself amongst the peasant slaves of Rome! There are hundreds of him… each one different. I am Spartacus. I am Spartacus. That's it. That's the answer. He hid himself so that we could each be him. Our own author. Our own authority.

FRANK *notices that* BARRY *has come back into the garage door.* FRANK *stops the film.* BARRY *comes forward to get his headphones.*

Silence.

Scene Nine

The Sergeant Returns to Arrest Shakespeare

Outside the garage, we hear the SERGEANT*'s car arrive. Headlights glare up the driveway into the garage. The flashing red or blue light. Then through a loud-hailer.*

SERGEANT. Charlton! Are you in there? Everyone stay right where you are. Each and every one of you. Where's Shakespeare, Charlton? Where is he? I know he's been down The Coach and Horses causing trouble, and then he's come back here, assaulted my brother and dragged him into this garage. Outside, on the floor, both of you!

The SERGEANT *approaches and talks with the audience as well as* FRANK *and* BARRY*, who sit, exactly like Kirk and Tony.*

What's he done? Taken off his fancy dress and hid himself amongst you lot? What are you all doing out at this time of night? Funny, is it? Right then! Ladies and gentleman of Oak Tree Close, Her Majesty's Government has no argument with you. Citizens of Kent you were and citizens of Kent you will be once again, but I'm warning you, the terrible punishment of a no-parking-tow-away zone in front of all your homes will be set aside on one condition only: you reveal to me the true identity of this troublemaker Shakespeare. I know he's sitting here amongst you lot. I know you know him.

The SERGEANT *shines his torch at the audience searching for Shakespeare.*

If I don't find him, Charlton, I'm going to come down on you like a tonne of bricks; I'll throw the book at you!

FRANK *begins to stand. Audience sometimes stood and took over here. Not bad if* FRANK *never gets to say it, like Kirk.*

BARRY (*standing*). I am Shakespeare.

SERGEANT. I'm arresting you for the…

FRANK. I am Shakespeare.

SERGEANT. Well then, I'll arrest you both unless there's anyone else who thinks they're Shakespeare. Who is that? Stand up, let me see you.

The Spartacus *film score rises to a triumphant end, as members of the audience stand and shout 'I am Shakespeare.'*

The End.

A little jig is recommended for the curtain call.

Parallelisms Between the Writing of Bacon and Shakespeare

From Shakespeare	*From Bacon's* **Promus**
…every Jack became a gentleman. (*Richard III*)	Every Jack would be a Lord.
…the latter end of a fray and the beginning of a feast. (*Henry IV, Part One*)	Better to come to the ending of a feast than to the beginning of a fray.
Good wine needs no bush. (*As You Like It*)	Good wine needs no bush.
…the strings of life Began to crack… (*King Lear*)	At length the string cracks.
Make use of thy salt hours. (*Timon of Athens*)	Make use of thy salt hours.
But I do love thee, and when I love thee not, Chaos is come again. (*Othello*)	Matter is not without a certain inclination and appetite to dissolve the world and fall back into the ancient chaos; but that the overswaying concord of things (which is represented by cupid or love) restrains its will and effect in that direction and reduces it to order. (*The Wisdom of the Ancients*)
…out of heaven's benediction com'st To the warm sun! (*King Lear*)	Out of God's blessing into the warm sun.

To hazard all our lives in one small boat. (*Henry VI, Part One*)	You are in the same ship.
Your bait of falsehood takes this carp of truth. (*Hamlet*)	Tell a lie to know the truth.
…the world on wheels. (*Two Gentlemen of Verona*)	The world runs on wheels.
Thought is free. (*The Tempest*)	Thought is free.
Fortune governed as the sea is by the moon. (*Henry IV, Part One*)	Fortune changes like the moon.
As if increase of appetite had grown, By what it fed on. (*Hamlet*)	If you eat appetite will come,
…can so young a thorn begin to prick? (*Henry VI, Part Three*)	A thorn is gentle when it is young.
What early tongue so sweet saluteth me? (*Romeo and Juliet*)	Sweet for the speech in the morning.

From *The Bacon-Shakespeare Question* by Nigel B. Cockburn.

Also published by Nick Hern Books

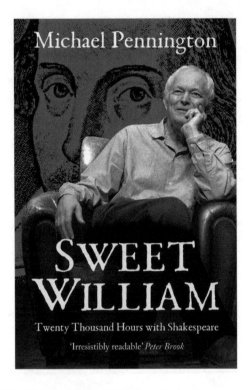

Michael Pennington's solo show about Shakespeare,
Sweet William, has been acclaimed throughout Europe and in the
US as a unique blend of showmanship and scholarship. In this
book, he deepens his exploration of Shakespeare's life and work
– and the connection between the two – that lies at its heart.

With practical analysis, wonderfully detailed and entertaining
interpretations of characters and scenes, and vivid reflections on
Shakespeare's theatre and ours, the result is a masterclass of the
most enjoyable kind for theatregoers, professionals, students
and anyone interested in Shakespeare.

£20 hardback · 336pp · ISBN 978-1-85459-568-3

Order from www.nickhernbooks.co.uk

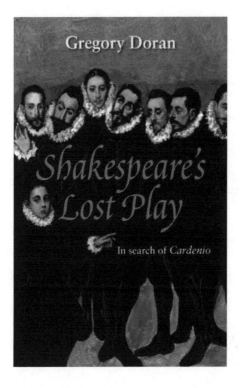

Gregory Doran's account of his quest to rediscover *Cardenio*,
the lost play written by Shakespeare and John Fletcher, is
a thrilling act of literary detection that takes him from the
Bodleian Library in Oxford, via Cervantes' Spain to the stage of
the Royal Shakespeare Company in Stratford.

Fully illustrated throughout, *Shakespeare's Lost Play* tells a
fascinating story, which, like the play itself, will engross
Shakespeare buffs and theatregoers alike.

£14.99 paperback · 288pp illustrated · ISBN 978-1-84842-208-7

Other Titles in this Series